Shell
Education

PreK-2

The *Gift* *of*
Playful
Learning
A Guide for Educators

Nadia Kenisha Bynoe   Angelique Thompson

Publishing Credits

Corinne Burton, M.A.Ed., *President and Publisher*
Aubrie Nielsen, M.S.Ed., *EVP of Content Development*
Kyra Ostendorf, M.Ed., *Publisher, Professional Resources*
Véronique Bos, M.S.Ed., *VP of Creative*
Cathy Hernandez, *Senior Content Manager*
Laureen Gleason, *Editor*
David Slayton, *Assistant Editor*
Kevin Pham, *Graphic Designer*

Image Credits: pp. 52, 75, 84 Shutterstock; All other images courtesy of Angelique Thompson and N. Kenisha Bynoe

A division of Teacher Created Materials
5482 Argosy Avenue
Huntington Beach, CA 92649
www.tcmpub.com/shell-education
ISBN 978-1-0876-4907-8
© 2023 Shell Educational Publishing, Inc.
Printed by: **418**
Printed in: **USA**
PO#: **PO9277**

To Xavier, the greatest gift I've ever been given. I am thankful that you share your love and brilliance with me every day.

—AT

To Kyrie, my nephew-son and all the little ones in my family who have inspired me to listen, respond, and teach with heart, thank you for transforming my pedagogical practice.

—NKB

Table of Contents

Acknowledgments

"One of the most vital ways we sustain ourselves is by building communities of resistance, places where we know we are not alone."

—bell hooks

We are forever grateful to the communities of love, support, and resistance we have been a part of. We cherish how you have made impressions on our hearts, minds, and souls. We are grateful to all the children who have taught us lessons that have transformed our thinking, and to the educators who have opened up their learning spaces so that we might be inspired, learn with them, and be provoked to change.

To our families, your gifts of love and courage have taught us about who we are and have instilled a sense of pride for our Bahamian and Vincentian heritages. We are especially thankful for mom (Janet), the "apple crumble" to our movements, who believed in our potential and provided insights and occasional edits along the way. To Garvey, whose patience and support for our work and writing time has been unwavering. You have willingly shared your wife with others and have shown unconditional love. We also extend our gratitude to our siblings whose educational experiences served as a catalyst to our own careers as educators.

To the inspiring mentor who was the first person to bring us together. There would be no "Kenisha and Angelique," had you not validated the work we were doing, supported our path to coaching, and encouraged us to always ask the questions "Why?" and "How?" Your inspiration has moved us to believe in the possibilities of transformative leadership. We are thankful for the nuggets of brilliance shared as we engaged in critical practitioner research under the guidance of Dr. Nicole West-Burns and inspirational leaders in the Toronto District School Board. With a focus on improving the achievement of Black learners, those research initiatives left an indelible mark on our learning journeys.

We are forever grateful to the two administrators who gave us the space to play with the possibilities at the beginning of our coaching careers, to share our learning and foster collaborative learning communities. To the centrally assigned principals and administrators who supported, provoked, challenged, learned, and led the way with us, we appreciate your insights and commitment to school improvement. We are mindful of an administrator who continues to challenge us to be excellent without excuses, a mantra that we strive to live by day by day. To the coordinators and centrally assigned principals in the Toronto District School Board Early Years Department, both past and present, your commitment to learners in the early years has ignited our passions and grounded our vision for young learners.

Last, but certainly not least, we want to acknowledge our critical friends—thank you for your support and for always sharing your honest and open perspectives whether sipping on bubble teas or enjoying a meal at Scaddabush.

Along our journey, we have been graced by the presence of many who have collectively inspired, provoked, and transformed our vision for learning. We are thankful for the gifts of love, support, wisdom, and encouragement you have all shared that have made *The Gift of Playful Learning* possible.

The Invitation

To those who honor children and view them as competent, capable, and curious;

To those who yearn to see themselves reflected and represented in the pages we turn and the spaces we share;

To those who value playful experiences that engage children;

To those who center themselves as risk takers in teaching and learning;

To those who are inspired to rethink and reimagine their teaching practices in ways that honor all learners;

To those who believe in thinking outside the box;

To those who love and are enchanted by learning—

We invite you on our journey as we unwrap the gift of learning.

Like a gift, the children we are entrusted with daily are precious and unique. And as they invite us to learn more about who they are and what they know through their actions, words, and thoughts, we too have opportunities to gift them with learning that is intentional, differentiated, and responsive to their strengths, needs, and wants.

This professional resource shares our journey with the children we have worked with and invites you to prepare gifts of learning inspired by the interests, curiosities, and lived experiences of the learners you work with. Gifts must be carefully selected and paired with intentional materials to uncover the possibilities of thinking and instruction. We highlight how you can plan and create these gifts through an exchange of learning and teaching that is deeply connected to the curriculum. We then guide you to invite children to unwrap these gifts, which are developed from their ideas, interpretations, and understandings.

Our own journey unfolded when we dared to dream and take risks in our thinking and learning. As we share this experience with you, we hope to inspire you to

- → transform your learning environment to become a landscape for play;

- → build creative spaces that speak to multiple identities, lived experiences, interests, and wonderings of learners, their families, and the community;

- → design playful experiences that lend themselves to deep thinking and critical learning;

- → gift children with opportunities that offer differentiated experiences;

- → engage children in purposeful learning that is designed with intention to provoke thought, curiosity, and wonder;

- → engage in dialogue with partners in learning; and

- → respond to observations that draw on children's capabilities.

We hope this resource motivates educators across the world to value play-based approaches as a vehicle for learning and thinking in the early years, which for the purposes of this book refers to children who are three to eight years old. The strategies, experiences, and resources we share support educators in creating spaces that engage, motivate, and sustain the thinking of children. In addition, this resource serves as a tool to support educators in differentiating learning experiences for children with diverse needs. Through instructional methods that honor play, we create pathways that are responsive to learners, building on their strengths, meeting their needs, and nurturing the growth they require to be successful academically.

Responding to the Invite and Wrapping the Gift

At the beginning of our own journey, we were invited to respond to learners' desires, which led us to believe in the possibilities of play. The children in our spaces pushed us to think in an unconventional manner. To center these learners' needs, we had to reimagine our programming.

As instructional coaches teaching in diverse spaces across the city of Toronto, we witnessed children communicating their needs differently. Some children displayed dissatisfaction within their learning spaces by escaping the classroom or demonstrating apathy, tears, explosive behaviors, or physical and emotional harm, which became normal conditions that made learning challenging. We realized these behaviors were the children's way of inviting us as educators to respond to what they were communicating about their needs for their learning environment. We were pressed to respond in one of two ways:

→ *Accept* their invitation and work intentionally to make shifts in our pedagogical approaches to teaching

or

→ *Decline* their invitation and hold fast to traditional approaches that were limiting children's competencies, allowing the tensions in the classroom to fester and escalate

Accepting the Invite

We decided to accept their invitation and to support the classroom educators in understanding the need and purpose for a shift in their programming. Through our observations and interpretations, we saw a need for more open, honest discussion with educators that would allow them to engage in the self-examination and reflection required to better recognize and address barriers facing their learners and school communities. Educators also began to question how play-based approaches for learning and culturally relevant pedagogy aligned with effective instruction.

We then had to tap into our teaching reservoir and draw on the pedagogical approaches and strategies we used in our own classrooms. The theory of culturally relevant pedagogy coined by Gloria Ladson-Billings (1994) inspired our foundational beliefs as educators. This foundation led us to offer learning that promoted excellence and success through high-yield strategies. As we navigated our instructional practice, we leveraged children's lived experiences and identities to shape a culture of belonging and contributing. We taught our youngest learners to critically evaluate the world around them.

As coaches, we noticed that children were presenting challenges, which led us to identify a number of gaps hindering the pursuit of learning success. Through our dialogue with each other, we began to share how the experiences we were observing deeply replicated historical legacies that resulted in success for some and marginalization for others. In our very own households, as we grew up, our families held high expectations and encouraged us to strive for excellence and be proud of our Caribbean heritages. However, we bore witness to the duality of education when the pathway to excellence was completely different for us than it was for our siblings. While we were able to successfully navigate the traditional system through acts of memorization, performance, and compliance, the expectations and instructional approaches delivered to our siblings presented great challenges and constrained the ways in which they learned. These tensions in achievement were deeply rooted within intersections of social identities such as race, gender, sexual orientation, ethnicity, ability, class, religion, and more (Crenshaw 1989).

Our curiosity about these tensions in learning served as a catalyst that steered our course as coaches. We firmly believe that it is our moral obligation as educators to shift the trajectory for learners. While their paths may be different, those paths do not have to be difficult. All children have a right to and deserve to learn in environments that honor culturally responsive practice through playful approaches.

As we accepted this invitation to make intentional shifts, we set out to create a *culture of thinking* and unlearn what was once traditionally assumed. We sought to undo the "worksheet pedagogy" that drove our own learning experiences and instead co-construct thinking and transform our learning environments. These shifts encouraged engagement, increased student voice, provoked thinking, and fostered a culture of higher expectations that supported students' success. Educators became more intentional in their instructional moves, were invigorated by learners' responses, and were able to support and address learners' diverse needs through differentiation. We then began to observe shifts in the behaviors of the children.

As we wrote this book, we faced even greater challenges due to the COVID-19 pandemic. In a time of change, we were compelled to improvise, adapt, and adjust. We were provoked to reimagine a new normal, one that would change spaces of learning in equitable and accessible ways. As we have continued to prioritize play, we have gained great lessons from our experiences that we share with you. In this book, we also consider the transformational approaches required to respond to how this time of uncertainty has affected children. Now more than ever, our systems crave pedagogical pivots that lead to transformation. We challenge you to envision new teaching practices, and we invite you to lean into this discomfort and embrace the lessons offered by the pandemic to shift toward new possibilities.

Unwrapping the Gift

The goal of this professional resource is to inspire educators with practical strategies for supporting learners with differentiated opportunities. Educators can rethink and reimagine their classroom instruction and programming in ways that offer all learners multiple entry points using culturally relevant and responsive resources, open-ended materials, and play. *The Gift of Playful Learning*

- → offers practical steps and considerations at the end of every chapter to guide educators along their journey;

- → embeds examples and experiences that share personal journeys, educator reflections, and photographs; and

- → offers a variety of planning templates and graphic organizers to support educators as they journey in this new learning.

This resource is for educators who want to foster a love of learning through intentional play offerings that consider all aspects of the curriculum and yield academic success. Throughout our work, we endeavor to appeal to diverse learners through play-based approaches that are integrated with culturally relevant and responsive teaching. This equitable approach, which we explore in the book, engages learners in playful opportunities and encourages them to think deeply and critically. While this book offers a comprehensive guide specifically for educators working in prekindergarten to second grade, it supports learning beyond these years as well. This book can also benefit system leaders and administrators who are working to transform school cultures and create sustainable structures for learning.

How to Unwrap This Gift

The sequence of this text follows a cyclical process that sees teaching and learning as iterative and moving in a nonlinear fashion (see figure 0.1).

Figure 0.1. The Learning Cycle

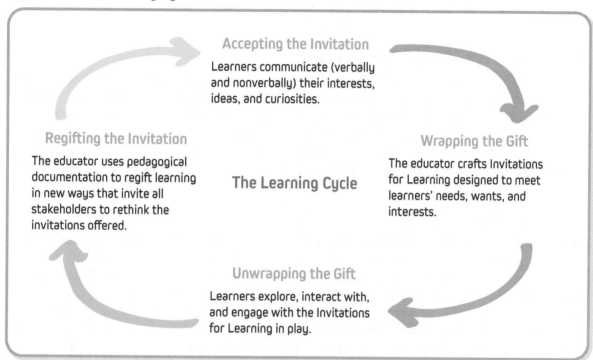

The chapters reflect the four aspects of the process of learning:

1. **Accepting the Invitation:** In the first portion of this text, we explore concepts that uncover how you can accept the invitations communicated by learners. Chapters 1 and 2 delve into the importance of play and the learning environment in connection to children's interests, ideas, and curiosities.

2. **Wrapping the Gift:** Chapters 3 and 4 outline how you should carefully consider what learners have communicated as you design opportunities to meet their interests, wants, and needs. We closely examine the purpose of open-ended materials and how to offer these materials within learning opportunities.

3. **Unwrapping the Gift:** In chapter 5, we offer guidelines for planning and strategies for unwrapping the gift of learning so that children can explore and engage with playful opportunities.

4. **Regifting the Invitation:** Finally, chapters 6 and 7 prepare you to use pedagogical documentation to regift learning in new ways that invite children and families to identify goals and next steps to rethink learning opportunities and programming.

Chapter 1: Exploring the Landscape of Play

This chapter uncovers the importance of play in creating joyful and purposeful experiences for diverse learners and shows how aligning play-based experiences with the curriculum offers rich learning for children and educators. We frame a continuum for play that moves from unintentional opportunities to purposeful learning experiences. The chapter provides an understanding of how play offers equitable entry points for learning and presents examples of how culture and identities have shifted the landscape of play.

Chapter 2: Creating Spaces That Speak

This chapter explores the power of the environment as a third teacher and how the elements of time, space, materials, and relationships can create equitable access points for learning. In this section, you are invited to consider how your personal biases and assumptions inform what is offered in your learning space. We uncover how classrooms speak and transfer the values that educators honor most. This chapter offers strategies for inviting children to share who they are and for creating opportunities where joy and learning can intersect through play.

Chapter 3: Playful Pieces

This chapter focuses on the theory of loose parts and how these playful pieces provoke learners to foster a *culture of thinking*. We uncover the importance of open-ended materials and the value they maintain in creating sustainable engagement, as these playful pieces invite learners to share stories that are deeply connected to their identities. This chapter provides strategies for scaffolding the use of loose parts in relation to text and for fostering learning opportunities in meaningful ways. You will learn about schematic play and how to intentionally connect loose parts to schemas (repetitive behaviors in play) to unpack biases and assumptions. We also make connections to the importance of open-ended materials as we reference Bloom's taxonomy. The chapter considers how to implement conditions for learning that allow for safe and intentional use of loose parts.

Chapter 4: Inviting Learning

In this chapter, we identify the elements of an Invitation for Learning. We define the difference between an activity, a provocation, and an Invitation for Learning. We give examples of Invitations for Learning and how they deepen connections to the curriculum and play. We consider how documentation can support and strengthen play-based experiences and redirect learning in purposeful ways. The chapter also shares misconceptions around Invitations for Learning and offers strategies for revitalizing offerings for play to reinvite and engage learners.

Chapter 5: Planning with Purpose

Our journey in learning continues as we explore key considerations for planning Invitations for Learning. You will gain a deeper understanding of how to plan Invitations for Learning that are reflective and responsive to children in an integrated and differentiated manner. We provide concrete examples, graphic organizers, and reflection questions to guide you in the planning process. We explore the worksheet continuum and revisit Bloom's taxonomy as it connects to planning Invitations for Learning, while considering how these invitations move children to think, analyze, create, and transfer skills.

Chapter 6: Playful Assessments

This chapter looks at protocols for pedagogical documentation and effective ways to record, collect, and analyze learning. We explore how documentation informs next steps in teaching practice through data gathered from playful classroom experiences. We also explore how to leverage documentation to consolidate learning and make connections to the curriculum. We reflect on how biases and assumptions inform our assessment practices and how to respond to, challenge, and extend thinking.

Chapter 7: Playful Partnerships

This last chapter explores the importance of partnerships and focuses on the power of engaging families as collaborators in learning. We consider meaningful ways to engage families in play opportunities that honor their lived experiences and capitalize on children's thinking. In this chapter, we uncover strategies for fostering partnerships that fuel play-based experiences. You will gain perspective on various forms of family engagement. We also offer practical ideas for inviting family members to serve as co-educators by noticing and naming learning to inform teaching practice.

As you navigate the chapters, key features within the text are included to support and inspire you in deepening your understanding of the material. Scenarios based on real classroom situations illustrate the implementation of key ideas in the text. "Playful Notes" share tips and strategies we have found helpful in our own practice. In addition, we have crafted questions to elicit deep reflection and discussion as you journey through the chapters. We have also included clarifying definitions and quotes that link to learning. And to help further recap ideas and connect them to practice, we include the following features in an **Additional Considerations** section:

→ **Missed Invitations:** Here we present misconceptions or missed opportunities along the learning journey. We address how to move through these missed invitations to be more responsive.

→ **Unraveling the Knots:** In our own practice, we have encountered tensions, challenges, or wonderings about the learning we have acquired and how it moves from theory to practice in seamless ways. This section unravels the knots that educators often contend with on the path to new discoveries.

→ **Pursuing the Gift:** In this section, we offer practical steps for you to implement in your own practice that align with the gifts of learning. These can be considered next steps for your own learning journey.

We close each chapter with **Gifts of Learning**. Here we revisit key ideas and concepts explored within the chapter. We review learning goals and consolidate the ideas that have been presented.

Join us as we unwrap the gift of learning.

Chapter 1

Exploring the Landscape of Play

It is mid-morning, and the school day is in full swing. We enter a space with a community of children who are confidently engaged in the intentional learning opportunities offered to them. As we stand at the entrance of this learning environment, a feeling of enchantment washes over us, and we are immediately invited into their world of play. As our eyes dance around, we see Invitations for Learning intricately placed within the classroom. Learners are captivated by a space that speaks to their interests, curiosities, identities, and intrigue—a space that validates their right to play.

In many learning environments, educators are shifting their teaching practices to provide programming that is inclusive of diverse learners, addressing ever-changing dynamics to nurture a myriad of interests, curiosities, and needs. Through play, learners' capabilities and competencies are actualized, and manifestations of learning become apparent.

Play is the greatest equalizer! Children play around the world, regardless of their lived experiences and social identities. Play transcends time and generations. As educators, we must appeal to the power of play. Play is fundamentally "an expression of freedom" (Gray 2008, para. 14)—a freedom void of stress and driven by a person's own intentions and desires.

What if play was honored as a right?

Play as a Right

The United Nations Convention on the Rights of the Child includes 54 articles upholding a universal standard that all children, at all times, without exception, need to thrive. While the UN Convention outlines a variety of basic human rights and freedoms entitled to children, it also values and honors the importance of play. If we consider play to be a right in our school communities, learning environments, and districts, we must consider what the right to play affords our learners within an institutional setting. We therefore propose these principles of the right to play (adapted from "Children's Rights to Read," published in 2018 by the International Literacy Association):

1. All children have the right to play and uncover *joy*, *imagination*, and *motivation*.

2. All children have the right to *choose* where and with whom they play.

3. All children have the right to *share* what they have learned from their global or local perspectives.

4. All children have the right to *access* open-ended materials that they can manipulate to enhance play.

5. All children have the right to play in a way that *mirrors* their lived experiences and identities, provides *windows* into the lives of others, and opens *doors* into their world.

6. All children have the right to play for extended periods of *time* that go uninterrupted.

7. All children have the right to play in a way that values different *expressions* for learning.

8. All children have the right to be *supported* in accessing play, based on their developmental needs.

When we promise such freedoms to our children, we liberate them from a *culture of doing* to a *culture of thinking*. When our spaces offer limited choices and rote or procedural tasks, they are focused on a culture of doing. However, when our spaces offer differentiated experiences that allow for multiple entry points in learning, they promote a culture of thinking. We invite possibilities without restriction, and we honor the voice of the child who yearns to discover the world through their own perspectives.

What Is Play?

There are many definitions of play. For us, "play is a vehicle for learning and rests at the core of innovation and creativity" (Ontario Ministry of Education 2016b, 18). Play encompasses joyful moments that are ignited through interactions, activity, or acts. Play elevates an experience by tickling the senses to appease a person's creativity, expressions, and inquisition. As identified by Friedrich Froebel, play represents the inner act of a child's thinking through outward expressions that require the manipulation of objects or the child's body (Nell et al. 2013). A child's learning potential is immeasurable when the child engages in play. Whether children are playing cooperatively, independently, or parallel with others, they demonstrate their understanding of the world in a variety of ways. Through play, children comprehend the world using their senses (Reimer et al. 2016).

Providing an opportunity for play means giving children the autonomy to express pleasure, demonstrate motivation, and create meaning through engagement. Children are innately drawn to play because it invites a freedom to interact with an inner consciousness in visible form. Visible manifestations of play are not just static physical creations; they also include outward expressions of movement and sound. Through play, we have an opportunity to tap into the infinite ways in which children symbolically express themselves. Children have an insatiable curiosity and desire to explore the world; with play as the vehicle, they are driven to take risks, reimagine possibilities, and share their own ideas. Play brings a flexibility of thought that gives children autonomy over their own learning and invites opportunities for exploration and expression.

The autonomy we refer to is the ability to make a decision—that is, the flexibility to choose whether to interact with others or simply play in solitude. Children must have agency over the materials they select for play, as the ability to "play is [an] intensely personal" (Mraz et al. 2016, 12) experience. How a child plays is equally as important as what is done during play. As children engage in acts of play, their play may shift in multiple contexts; a child may express a desire to play alone, cooperatively with another child, or side by side in a parallel way (White 2012).

Types of Play

When we hear the word *play*, specific imagery comes to mind that connects us to our own lived experiences and identities. While interpretations of play differ, it is important to highlight that play comes in a variety of forms. Bob Hughes (2002) has identified 16 types of play (see figure 1.1). When we observe play, we notice the types of play that unfold for each child; through the information we gather, we come to understand that play embodies specific characteristics. We also recognize the fluid and overlapping nature of the play types, and we see the value in creating environments that foster rich play opportunities.

Figure 1.1. Types of Play

Imaginative Play	Mastery Play
Children use their imaginations to act out experiences that would not apply in the real world. *Example:* Pretending it is snowing inside.	Children try to control their physical environments through play. *Example:* Digging tunnels in sand.
Creative Play	**Exploratory Play**
Children explore and use their own ideas and theories to create something. *Example:* Using materials to create a musical composition.	Children explore objects that are in their spaces and use their senses to process and make sense of new information. *Example:* Dragging hands over materials, then smelling them.
Fantasy Play	**Socio-dramatic Play**
Children allow their creativity and imagination to be free as they conjure ideas and concepts. *Example:* Pretending to be an astronaut.	Children act out real-life experiences that are based on their prior knowledge. *Example:* Pretending to shop at the mall.
Communication Play	**Locomotor Play**
Children play through ideas, songs, rhymes, poetry, and words. *Example:* Telling jokes.	Children engage in a world of movement. *Example:* Playing freeze tag.
Rough-and-Tumble Play	**Dramatic Play**
Children are in physical contact with objects or with other children. *Example:* Rolling down a hill.	Children dramatize and act out roles that are assigned or invented. *Example:* Playing a dentist who is caring for a patient.
Symbolic Play	**Recapitulative Play**
Children transform objects, actions, and ideas into new representations. *Example:* Using a stick as a wand.	Children explore history, ancestry, rituals, and stories connected to culture and identity. *Example:* Using sand to reenact a prayer ritual.
Role Play	**Social Play**
Children take on a role that moves beyond domestic or personal roles associated with other types of dramatic play. *Example:* Pretending to use a phone.	Children engage in social or interactive play that follows expectations and rules. *Example:* Playing "Red Light, Green Light."
Deep Play	**Object Play**
Children take risks that are connected to their mood. *Example:* Overcoming the fear of climbing a tall tree or jumping to another surface.	Children play with an object that involves hand-eye coordination. *Example:* Using a paintbrush to paint.

Source: Adapted from Encourage Play (n.d.); play type information from Hughes (2002).

Characteristics of Play

Everywhere around the world, at any given time, children exhibit characteristics of play that offer learning to us as observers. Through playful expressions, children reveal their skills within the developmental domains. Play serves as the optimal context for learning. Gray (2008) and White (2012) share several characteristics that define play:

1. Play can be joyful and liberating.

2. Play is self-directed and offers children choice.

3. The process within play is more valued than the product.

4. Several mental processes guide play.

5. Play is imaginative and non-literal.

6. Play is emotionally, physically, and mentally engaging.

Why Is Play Important?

Play is a powerful educational tool that provides multiple entry points for learners to access curriculum content. Through play, young children develop foundational skills that support social, emotional, cognitive, and physical growth. Early childhood development depends on integrated approaches to learning that support all subject areas. Math, science, literacy, and the arts are interconnected—and what better way to merge these disciplines than through play?

Neurologically, as children engage in play, the brain creates pathways that support the development of many skills. These pathways create a foundation for future learning, behavior, and health.

> Children have very flexible brains. Scientists describe this as "brain plasticity." The nature of children's brain structure allows them to actually see more, hear more, and experience feelings more intensely than adults. They take in large amounts of sensory information, and they investigate and act on sensory input; they form brain pathways for all their future learning and capabilities. (Curtis and Jaboneta 2019, 16)

Research shows us that play is beneficial for childhood development. If we are to offer play-based approaches to teaching, we must first know why it is so important. We believe play is the best avenue for learning because it supports development in holistic ways. Figure 1.2 shows the multiple ways in which play can support children.

Our approach to play contradicts widespread misconceptions that children need to gain specific skills at earlier ages; instead, play lays the foundation for children to be able to engage in skills when it is appropriate for them to do so.

Figure 1.2. How Play Supports Children's Growth

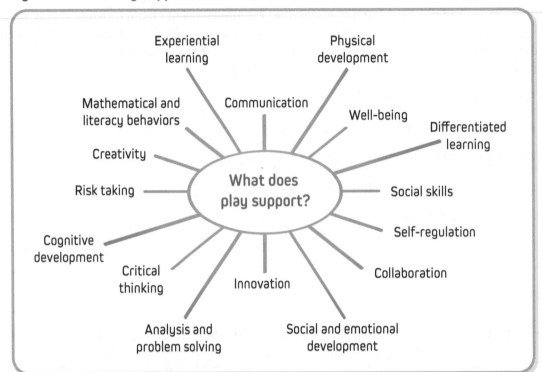

Susan Stacey, the author of *Inquiry-Based Early Learning Environments*, confirms that the most efficient way to develop foundational skills for learning in childhood development is through play-based learning. She notes:

> The nature of a play-based, emergent program is to inquire, probe, experiment, and mess about. Through this process, we encounter unexpected delights, develop our own theories about how children learn and how we might teach, and, if we are observant and vigilant, arrive at the questions and ideas of children which—when taken seriously—will lead to deeper learning through engagement. (Stacey 2019, 142)

Play-based learning invites us to think about the power it fosters as it transcends fun to provoke critical thinking, problem solving, communication, collaboration, and more. In play, children naturally explore the global competencies that will equip them for twenty-first-century learning, which will in turn develop the skills necessary for our ever-changing world. To prepare learners for the future, we must offer opportunities through play that help them develop the skills necessary to be successful.

> There is no better place to develop a child's imagination than in play. When children engage in imaginative play, not only do they develop their creativity; they learn to be flexible thinkers, and they develop core social skills, such as negotiation, collaboration, and empathy. (Mraz et al. 2016, 6)

While we consider what learners need for the future, we must hold true to what they need now, without losing perspective of how play strengthens these needs. Our learning environments should embed developmentally appropriate and intentional playful experiences that tap into the curriculum.

Play Is Therapeutic

As we write this book, the COVID-19 pandemic has left the world in crisis. During this time, families have undergone immense hardship, stress, and loss while navigating the unpredictability of a global emergency. To support children as they continue to experience the impact of the pandemic, play should be centered at the heart of learning. Through playful interactions with open-ended materials, children can access their emotions more freely. The liberating nature of play allows a child to navigate their stresses in a healthy manner and creates avenues for children to build empathy in a time of crisis. "Play also helps to develop an individual's stress response system" (Mraz et al. 2016, 13). As educators, we can leverage play to support our learners. Children can self-regulate their emotions and determine strategies for coping with their anxieties. Because play involves choice, it gives children a platform to make their thinking visible and to share their voices. Play amplifies their stories, curiosities, and theories, interrupting adult-centric views.

The pandemic has propelled us as coaches and educators to re-envision a counternarrative to traditional teaching and learning approaches. Educators around the world have been challenged to reimagine a new normal, one that would transform spaces of learning in equitable and accessible ways. In our own programs, we have prioritized play to meet the developmental needs of all learners.

What Are Play-Based Approaches to Learning?

Play is pedagogy; it is *the* approach that can uphold teaching practices and honor children's capabilities as they manipulate open-ended materials in pursuit of knowledge. When we invite play and curriculum to merge, we create a harmonious relationship. Play-based teaching allows every child to have multiple opportunities to express thought, theory, and prior knowledge to differentiate learning. The educator's role is to reveal the connections that can be made between play and teaching practices. Using play, educators leverage the curriculum to meet the strengths and needs of every learner.

Five Key Principles of Play-Based Approaches to Learning

To consider how play-based learning might inspire our learning spaces, let's explore these fundamental principles (Ontario Ministry of Education, n.d.):

1. Play is recognized as a child's right, and it is essential to the child's optimal development.

2. All children are viewed as competent, curious, capable of complex thinking, and rich in potential and experience.

3. A natural curiosity and a desire to explore, play, and inquire are the primary drivers of learning among young children.

4. The learning environment plays a key role in what and how a child learns.

5. In play-based learning programs, assessment supports the child's learning and autonomy as a learner.

Play-Based Learning Uncovered

1. **Play is recognized as a child's right, and it is essential to the child's optimal development.**

   As we noted previously, play is a right through which our learners communicate their wants, intentions, and needs. When we carefully observe what children say and do in play, we gain insight into how to support their learning in connection with our teaching instruction. Too often, play is juxtaposed with work and viewed as a reward but not valued as an integral core of classroom instruction. We have observed educators asking children to complete worksheets, with play following only as a reward for finishing this work.

   When play is seen as a right for children, educators realize that "play *is* the work of children." In our schools, districts, and communities, we try to address necessities for survival, such as food, shelter, water, clothing, and education. How might play fit in with these other needs? To reframe play as a fundamental need, we must make shifts in our pedagogy. "Play is not a luxury. It is a necessity" (Mraz et al. 2016, 2).

2. **All children are viewed as competent, curious, capable of complex thinking, and rich in potential and experience.**

   Our views about children lie at the heart of a play-based learning approach. In adopting such an approach to pedagogy, we must consider children through an asset-based lens. When we as educators view children following this principle, our instructional approaches will also reflect this perspective. When we speak to their competencies, we see them as children who are capable of inquiring, investigating, communicating, problem solving, creating, and more. The cultural currencies of children's views, experiences, and identities offer a wealth of knowledge for educators.

   In the play-centric classroom, reciprocal learning emerges, and the voices of children and their families are amplified. Educators who adopt this stance will see the learning process ignited by children's active engagement in collaborating, co-constructing, and contributing. When we view children as proficient in play, this becomes a priority in our planning; the discourse of play shifts and disrupts traditional notions of children as passive consumers.

When we hear this:	Educators who affirm an asset view of children might respond:
"My learners aren't ready for painting; they will just make a big mess."	By offering multiple mediums for children to explore in artistic ways and leveraging challenges encountered as an opportunity for communal problem solving.
"They need to work on their printing. They don't know how to write their names."	By providing opportunities for learners to develop their fine-motor skills through painting, intentional playdough experiences, writing utensils, and more.
"I have to show them how to play with these things, or else they won't do what I need them to."	By gathering insight, learning from, and honoring the multiple ways children approach the materials and invitations, which inform next steps in planning.
"They perform better with pencil-and-paper tasks."	By observing what learners are most interested in and prioritizing these expressions when planning opportunities.

3. **A natural curiosity and a desire to explore, play, and inquire are the primary drivers of learning among young children.**

Children have an insatiable curiosity to understand the marvels of the world, driven by their senses. This drive quenches their thirst to attain knowledge in meaningful ways. "Play is the overarching context for the transactions that occur between children and their materials" (Compton and Thompson 2018, 18). Interpreting the world requires a desire to wonder, tinker, and inquire. "Play is an activity enjoyed for its own sake. It is our brain's favorite way of learning and maneuvering" (Ackerman 1999, 11).

A child's choice in play leads the way for our pedagogy to meet inner workings that are outwardly displayed. As educators, we are challenged to be responsive to such desires through feedback, provocation, questioning, observation, powerful interactions, and explicit instruction in a whole group, a small group, or individually. Shifting our thinking requires a reciprocal exchange of information from educator to learner and from learner to educator. This reciprocal approach invites us to honor learning that is not solely teacher directed but values children's voices in a reflective and responsive manner.

Play is a teaching approach that demands the willingness to tinker, explore, investigate, and discover. Play involves learning that is bound to the curriculum and invites integration of all subject matters in ways that cannot be isolated or pulled apart. "Play is its own method of instruction" (Mraz et al. 2016).

4. **The learning environment plays a key role in what and how a child learns.**

The learning environments that we aim to foster should create a sense of belonging, safety, comfort, and familiarity. These environments promote a welcoming space where learners can identify with their experiences and use cultural currencies to develop their images of self in relation to space. Equitable spaces are flexible and require strong connections to the elements of time, space, materials, and relationships. A space that functions effectively with all four elements responds to children's voices intentionally and in a way that extends thinking to inform the design of the environment. "Because play is safe and familiar, children feel free to take risks and try on new learning" (Mraz et al. 2016, 6). A space that supports challenge, flexibility, creativity, and collaboration is designed and negotiated by both the learners and the educator. This environment is constructed to differentiate learning and individualize instruction.

5. **In play-based learning programs, assessment supports the child's learning and autonomy as a learner.**

The autonomous nature of play affords children the liberty to demonstrate their thinking in a variety of forms. Through this liberating act, children demonstrate what they know, and educators (along with families) use what children say, do, and represent to analyze and develop next steps for teaching. As we peer into these windows that reveal experiences, developmental needs, and personal reflections, we come to a newfound understanding of each child.

Educators are inquirers who uncover the authentic connections that children are making to curriculum through play. Assessment within play imparts more than just knowledge and understanding; rather, it transfers the child's use of their skills and competencies in multiple contexts for learning.

Play Continuum

A space that embraces play-based approaches to learning cultivates opportunities for learners and educators to participate in reciprocal roles in the learning process. Figure 1.3 illustrates the continuum of play in the classroom, with the center highlighting the optimal conditions for play to flourish within a learning environment.

Figure 1.3. Continuum of Play

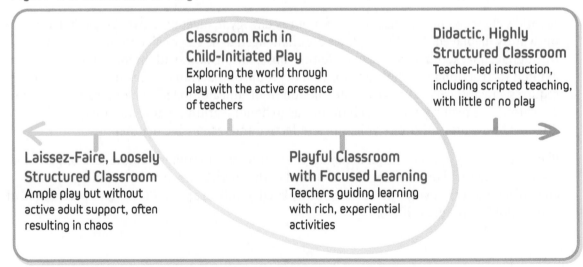

Source: Miller and Almon (2009, 8). Used with permission.

Through play-based environments, we as educators invite learners to initiate their own thinking through play. As we become attuned to children's needs and curiosities, we layer their play experiences with materials and opportunities that stimulate their thinking to attain curriculum goals. The most effective playful approaches live in the center of the continuum, where learners are exploring the classroom and provoking their thinking, while the educator is guiding, introducing, and extending new information.

Play-based learning demands that we as educators establish a rapport with children to find the best teaching methods to meet their needs. Play is a stance taken on by the educator to encompass all subject areas. It is not seen as a designated time in the day but is fluidly embedded in all areas of instruction. When we adopt a play-based stance, we aim to instruct in playful ways with the use of materials. In whole-group, small-group, or individual learning experiences, our instructional practices are founded on play. Play permeates instruction to invite the disciplines to dance with one another in the hands of learners. Rather than separating play from "academics," playful learning flows throughout the day and meets all learners on their pedagogical journeys.

Playing with Purpose

As we invite children to play, we learn to provide meaningful experiences that serve as pathways to uncover thinking and learning. Children play *with, in,* and *on* purpose as they problem-solve and work through tensions in thinking to elicit new possibilities.

When children play *with* purpose, they hold an intention in mind that manifests before them through the manipulation of open-ended materials. A child who is eager to enter play and has a vision of what they want to create or do draws close to the materials that will allow them to see their vision come to life. For example, Xavier shares with the educator that he wants to design the "Big Ben Clock Tower" and moves toward the blocks offered to actualize his idea.

Playing *in* purpose allows children to explore and investigate, and over time, to experience meaningful moments that reveal new and intentional ways to use open-ended materials. Learners discover the properties of the materials as they understand their multidimensional purposes. Understanding a material's functions leads children to an intended purpose that expands as they determine how their vision should be represented in play. For example, an educator observes a child in play manipulating seashells and asks what they are doing. The child replies, "I don't know." Later, the educator revisits the child, who then is able to share, "I used the shells in the sand and blue gems. The people are my family. We have family in the Bahamas."

Finally, playing *on* purpose allows children to capture the thinking offered in another child's previous experience or through the educator's strategic questioning; the new information gathered from previous play experiences now redefines the very act of play, and the intended outcome is then imagined. For example, a child shares that they are continuing a story that was read in class. Another child joins the play experience, and the children use materials to act out a new ending to the story. This then changes the experience in play for the initial learner. As another example, a child is exploring metal materials and notices that they create sound; the educator provokes thinking by saying, "Let me repeat what you shared, and I want you to listen closely and tell me what you notice." The child shares that they notice a pattern and begins to create a musical composition using rhythmic patterns. The educator's questioning has shifted the thinking of the learner.

The acts of playing *with, in,* and *on* purpose are intersectional and build on one another to drive purpose in environments that foster play. "No one has ever watched a child intent in [their] play without being made aware of the complete merging of playfulness and seriousness" (Cuffaro 1995, 85).

Culturally Relevant Pedagogy in Play

Play offers equitable entry points for unleashing all learners' potential to succeed. In early years environments, children gain a sense of belonging and connectedness informed by their social identities. Notions of who they are and how they see the world shape their narratives in play. Play is a deeply personal experience, and when children interact with their peers, materials, and resources, we realize that each moment reflects the inner life of the child. They share intimate stories about themselves, gain perspective of others, and consider the possibilities of what might be.

Gloria Ladson-Billings invites us to see how culturally relevant pedagogy can shape and influence our perspectives in teaching and learning. She stresses that culturally relevant pedagogy must provide a way for students to maintain cultural integrity while succeeding academically (Ladson-Billings 1995). To engage in this work of sustaining cultural identities and high expectations, we first must unpack the definition of *culture*. We can use the following interpretation to guide our thinking:

> Culture goes much deeper than typical understandings of ethnicity, race and/or faith. It encompasses broad notions of similarity and difference and it is reflected in our students' multiple social identities and their ways of knowing and of being in the world. (Ontario Ministry of Education 2013, 8)

It is also important to note that culture is not necessarily understood in homogenous ways; it shifts depending on location, context, space, and time. Immediately, when we are offered the word *culture*, we ascribe our preconceived ideas to our interpretations, such as food, music, clothing, and so on. While these very visible representations of culture might resonate most with educators and often drive their programming, we invite you to interrogate your understanding of culture to include visible and nonvisible cultural identities.

Teaching with "surface culture" (tangible expressions of culture such as food, music, art) as the sole entity denies the complexities of identity and how our own social location shapes and influences how we see others. *Social location* refers to the many identities held by an individual. When we begin to explore our own social identities, to consider our race, ethnicity, language, culture, gender, sexual orientation, religion, ability, education, age, and more, we realize that certain identities we hold provide advantages, while others can disadvantage us in social contexts. So what does this mean for us in the context of education?

While we want to honor celebratory practices of culture, we also must honor the complexities of cultural identities to better understand the communities and families we serve in multiple ways. We must not approach culturally relevant teaching from an ethnocentric perspective. In this we mean that we must strive to ensure our own cultural identities do not bias, privilege, or harm the development of children who are beginning to create their own sense of self. Culturally relevant pedagogy invites educators to shift their dispositions around teaching from a deficit perspective about identities to an asset-based approach.

Deeper understandings of culture require us to listen, observe, ask questions, and respond to teaching with relevance and vigilance. Culturally relevant pedagogy commands us to critique societal norms and engage learners to think critically while centering the lived realities of learners, their families, and their communities. In doing this, culture becomes the catalyst for learning in ways that are meaningful, engaging, and authentic. By affirming the cultural capital offered by all stakeholders, educators appeal to learners and engage them in ways that allow for deeper connections to the curriculum. This pedagogical approach outlines three principles: *high expectations*, *cultural competence*, and *critical consciousness*. Figure 1.4 details how play-centric learning environments support these three tenets.

Figure 1.4. How Play-Centric Learning Environments Support Culturally Relevant Pedagogy

Principles of Culturally Relevant Pedagogy	How Play-Centric Learning Environments Support These Principles
High expectations shift educators' views of learners from passive consumers or "blank slates" to being competent and capable of excellence. Instruction is founded on high-yield strategies that prioritize achievement for all. Children and educators hold high expectations for themselves and others. They are entrusted to choose academic pathways of excellence.	Play-based learning recognizes that all learners are on a journey to excellence. Children can demonstrate their strengths by differentiating learning and presenting their "work" in divergent ways. In play, children are recognized for their efforts and successes. Play yields understanding for children in an integrated fashion that considers many subject areas. Educators gain more assessment and information about a child's learning as the approach merges multiple disciplines in one playful experience.
Cultural competence privileges the lived realities of children and honors what they bring to the educational institution. Culture is the compass that guides learning for both educators and children. It surpasses surface knowledge of culture, such as celebrations, and leads to a more responsive understanding of the cultural identities that exist within school communities.	Play welcomes the multiple perspectives of children as they weave cultural narratives of their lives. It summons learners' strengths and empowers them to make choices in play that center around their knowledge of the world. As educators and learners interact with one another, the materials, and the learning environment, they create a connectedness that is founded on an essence of humanity.
Critical consciousness challenges educators to engage learners in discourse that critiques injustices and inequities that exist in the world. Through intentional learning experiences, children gain the skills needed to become critical citizens of the future. Once educators and learners identify an injustice, they have a responsibility to act on it.	Play provides the most favorable conditions for learners to naturally engage in dialogue, critical thinking, and problem solving. As children engage with others and assume alternate roles through play, they gain perspectives of others. Educators listen intently to children and observe what is revealed through play. Our biases and assumptions as educators influence how we perceive play experiences. Learners also hold biases and assumptions while engaged in play. Critically conscious educators carefully consider how to intentionally disrupt this thinking in ways that foster new understandings for themselves and children. Learners become agents of change who interrupt norms, values, and dispositions that align with the dominant narrative.

A paradigm shift occurs when we marry play with culturally relevant teaching—learning spaces not only honor play, but also seamlessly infuse the identities and experiences of children into learning opportunities while challenging injustices. When play and culturally relevant teaching merge, we see a seamless interconnection of the three tenets that supports pedagogy. Culturally relevant pedagogy lives within our everyday play-based programming.

We invite you to explore the following scenario (shown in the photos above) and consider the integrated nature of the three principles as it emerges through a playful experience:

> *Ben is observed lining up wooden blocks in a sequence of pillars; these serve as anchors for platforms that arch the base of what appears to be a bridge. As he begins to build a ramp, he excitedly points and says, "Vietnam, small bridges." The educator begins to ask questions to prompt more communication, as she supports Ben's acquisition of the English language. In play, Ben begins to share his journey from Vietnam, his country of birth, to the United States and Canada. As Ben continues to build his bridge, he points and articulates, "That is the bridge to the US from Canada. It is big!" The educator then places a blue piece of fabric on the floor, and Ben shares, "That is the river under the bridge. Vietnam." He grabs a wooden peg person and moves it across the bridge, exclaiming, "Coming to Canada!"*

> *Another child enters the play experience and states, "Why are you in my country?" and says, "You can't come!" as he places a red block to prevent passage over the bridge.*

> *The educator questions the child further to gain more insight into his thinking. This interaction provokes the educator to engage in thoughtful lessons and Invitations for Learning to honor Ben's experience while disrupting notions around belonging.*

Following this encounter, the educator accepted the invitation by gifting learners with the following opportunities:

→ Offering intentionally selected texts that highlight the narratives of families who have journeyed to new countries: *All Are Welcome* by Alexandra Penfold, *Where Are You From?* by Yamile Saied Méndez, *Lubna and Pebble* by Wendy Meddour, and *Out* by Angela May George

→ Sharing videos about families who have journeyed to new countries: *Jamie Lo, Small and Shy* by Lillian Chan and *From Far Away* by Shira Avni and Shareen El-Haj Daoud

→ Engaging in learning about Indigenous people who inhabited the land long before settlers arrived

→ Offering photos of different types of bridges from around the world that connect to the cultural heritages of learners in the classroom and beyond

→ Creating an Invitation for Learning using the book *Out*, which is a story about immigration, inviting learners to share their stories and make connections to the text (see figure 1.5 on the next page)

→ Reestablishing learning conditions through a series of classroom meetings around the question "How might we make others feel welcome?"

→ Inviting families to share their experiences of challenge, perseverance, and courage as they immigrated to Canada

→ Exploring notions of inclusion by unpacking common narratives of who might be welcomed into the country and who might not

→ Writing letters to their local representative and school administrators that suggested ideas for how communities and individuals might welcome newcomer families to Canada or the school

From this small moment captured within play, the educator crafted multiple experiences that were layered over time to address a number of ideas that emerged.

Figure 1.5. An Invitation for Learning That Honors a Child's Experience

How Does This Experience Connect to Culturally Relevant Pedagogy?

In this experience, we observed that learners were entrusted with open-ended materials to share personal accounts of their lives. The educator provided an independent opportunity for young learners to interact and share their views of the world around them. The conversation was not immediately interrupted; instead, an exchange occurred between learners, and questions were used to draw more conclusions. This playful experience required the educator to uphold high expectations for learners by exploring the social tensions that arose in play. The educator's view of the children's capacity to engage in learning around complex ideas such as immigration, refugee experiences, and settler privileges resulted in an intentional selection of text.

Acknowledging families and children as co-educators shifted the power dynamic, and reciprocal learning ensued as all stakeholders constructed meaning together. Providing space for learners to have the liberty to be agents of change and voice their opinions within their local and global communities was transformative and empowering. In this scenario, we see how the three tenets of culturally relevant pedagogy are inseparable and are integrated with intricacy.

How Does This Experience Connect to the Curriculum?

Play is integrative! It allows us to observe how the disciplines of science, math, literacy, and the arts meld into a harmonious experience for learning. As children play, they apply conceptual understandings that intertwine with the three tenets of culturally relevant pedagogy (high expectations, cultural competence, and critical consciousness), as well as the curriculum.

In the scenario, interaction with the invitations for learning uncovered extensive literacy learning opportunities:

→ Children made deep connections to text while engaging in early literacy behaviors that challenged them to consider different perspectives, engage in visualization, and infer.

→ Oral stories emerged as the children interacted with the materials, demonstrating their understanding of narratives and personal recounts. This sparked an opportunity for further development, with educator support, of storytelling and personal recounts.

→ Children participated in authentic writing opportunities that supported their development of voice and purpose.

→ Children expanded their repertoire of vocabulary words while crafting persuasive text that represented their desire for social change.

The photos of the bridges offered inspiration and challenged the children to embark on new engineering and design challenges. Mathematical concepts of symmetry, stability, and measurement appeared within play, and the educator was able to capitalize on these teachable moments during whole-group instruction. As the children manipulated the blocks, they began to notice the dimensions of each piece with more precision as they problem-solved and tested their theories through measurement, prediction, and estimation and questioned their way to new knowledge. The artistry that emerged from the architecture in play beautifully complemented the cultural aesthetic that was infused into their designs.

The educator optimized learning by meeting learners' needs through whole-group, small-group, and independent instruction. The assessments gathered through play informed the strategies and next steps for learning. Through the strategy of noticing and naming the learning (see chapter 6), the educator used documentation captured from play to respond to, challenge, and extend thinking.

Uncovering Biases and Assumptions

Play allows educators to understand the cultural experiences of learners while also providing us with access to engage in challenging conversations that unearth the realities of ableism, ageism, sexism, racism, classism, homophobia, transphobia, and many other topics. Play is the language that speaks to learners in accessible ways, and it invites exploration, investigation, and communication that lead to social advocacy.

While some might argue that children are too young to engage in topics of such complexity, we as educators must understand that learners are developing key characteristics of identity. Louise Derman-Sparks and Julie Edwards (2020) explain that fostering a child's sense of self demands an environment that cultivates esteem building and allows children to affirm who they are without claiming superiority over others. Derman-Sparks and Edwards share these key characteristics of child identity development:

→ Young children are curious about their own and others' physical and cultural characteristics.

→ Children begin to construct a personal sense of self and multiple social identities.

→ Children learn about their own and others' social identities through both overt and covert messages.

→ Young children are learning about who is and is not important.

→ Children try to make sense of all that they see and hear.

→ Young children develop pre-prejudice as they absorb negative attitudes, misinformation, and stereotypes about various aspects of human diversity.

→ Children begin to construct their own versions of who belongs in their country.

→ Children begin to be aware of power dynamics linked to social identities. (2020, 12–16)

When these identity characteristics reveal themselves through play, educators must use what occurs as an opportunity for dialogue and questioning, and intentionally plan for learning.

We believe there is insurmountable evidence of the power, purpose, and benefits of play. While endless resources sing its praises, play continues to be viewed in irreverent ways. In society's push for productivity and efficiency, academic rigor is pressed on our learners through instructional approaches that are neither developmentally appropriate nor effective. Pedagogy that privileges the regurgitation and memorization of facts and the consumption of knowledge in rigid and monolithic ways has infiltrated our school systems. Many educators, administrators, schools, and districts view play as an ineffective pedagogical approach, despite the evidence.

Jaye Thiel describes the impact of such thinking: "When educators say a child 'can't play' or engage in particular narratives because those narratives aren't part of the privileged discourse, a powerful and marginalizing silence takes place in the classroom" (2014, 13). According to Kristine Mraz, Alison Porcelli, and Cheryl Tyler:

> When we impose our personal, adult opinions on children's words
> created in play, we send the message that certain children do not
> belong because the desires and questions they bring to play are
> uncomfortable for adults. Yet, with or without our approval, children
> use play as a way to make sense of the world. (2016, 22)

Play provides a foundation for skills that are sustainable and prepare our learners to be critical, global citizens of the future. If we truly view learners as competent and capable, we must honor their play pursuits by delving into topics that are culturally attuned.

We must also interrogate our experiences of play and understand what factors bias our beliefs about play and how they have influenced our understanding. Perceptions of play-based learning are often tainted by our interpretations, which are informed by our culture, identity, and socialization. We therefore must gather information through documentation of what learners say, do, and represent. As described in this chapter, play provides equitable entry points for all learners to share the language of joy, learning, and development.

Our learners, families, and communities should be centered in our systems of education. In their playful pursuits, learners invite us to explore authentic experiences—whether positive or negative—that highlight their beliefs, assumptions, and cultural identities. Once we have been presented with this invitation, we can begin to purposefully wrap a wondrous gift intricately designed for teaching and learning.

Additional Considerations

Missed Invitations

As we have explored the landscape of play, we have discovered that this rigorous journey can present us with obstacles and misgivings. The invitations that learners offer to us may not always reveal themselves immediately; sometimes they are made clear in hindsight. We must then recover our path by taking up the opportunities we have missed or the misconceptions that have arisen. We invite you to consider how these misconceptions or missed opportunities emerge within the context of play:

Missed Invitation 1: Playful experiences evoke only joy.

Play is often a pleasurable experience, and we can bear witness to the joy it elicits for children. However, through play, learners might also express situations that are deeply rooted in emotional distress, trauma, or discomforting acts. Play can be a therapeutic approach for learners to express their traumas and share freely in uninhibited ways. What might this mean for us in an educational context when we limit such opportunities for our learners to play out their inner stories of distress?

Missed Invitation 2: Play is just for fun.

This idea is deeply connected to one rooted in the instructional approach of a laissez-faire stance, which was shown in the continuum of play earlier in this chapter (see figure 1.3). The idea that play produces chaos and limited opportunities for learning stems from a rigid misunderstanding of the potential play has for all the developmental domains. Play-based approaches to learning encourage children to think deeply as they demonstrate their knowledge in very interconnected ways. In this chapter, we have explored how play supports cognitive, physical, social, and emotional development. When educators become more attuned to noticing the potential that play brings to their programming, their ideas shift beyond surface understandings of play as "just fun."

Missed Invitation 3: Play is performative.

Play-based learning is fun and also serious work for children. We find that educators may involve themselves in play for the sake of hearing and seeing what they want to see. A performative undercurrent drives such practices in play. When we instead acknowledge that, as Albert Einstein once said, "play is the highest form of research," we value the importance of assessment through playful experiences. Educators may intend to gather more thinking, but if they want to document a moment in play that they have missed recording, they may ask the learners to re-create what they have already done authentically during play. This not only interrupts the learning but also leads learners to *perform* in play. When classroom conditions have been set up this way, we often see children replicating what they feel is pleasing to the educator, as opposed to being uninhibited. They stay within the border of what is expected of them.

Missed Invitation 4: Play does not require collaboration with learners, families, and communities.

We encourage you to invite playful opportunities throughout the day, whether in large-group, small-group, or individual settings. Play-based learning should always be purposeful and planned with the intention of extending, challenging, or responding to thinking. We must value the collaborative moments that present themselves in playful pursuits. When we define collaboration, we consider not only the learners but also the provoking that occurs when educators co-construct learning with children to build on preconceived concepts. We depend on the learning exchange that occurs between families, learners, and educators.

Unraveling the Knots

Playful pedagogy encourages us to reflect on the challenges, wonderings, and tensions that unsettle our teaching practice. As we center learners and the gifts they present, we receive the invitation to reform, reshape, and rethink what we once conventionally assumed. We must tease out the tensions, challenges, and wonderings to unveil the marvels of learning for ourselves and children. We ask you to consider how play is or is not honored in your spaces. Join us in unraveling the knots we have discovered along this journey:

Knot 1: Play is used as a reward that must be earned and is not valued as an instructional approach.

In play, the brain builds connections. It behooves us to use play as a foundation *for* learning, as it cannot be separated *from* learning. In our observations of learning environments, we have seen that play is often "given" to learners if they have completed the "real work" at the table. If the educator believes a child to be "deserving," they then gift play to that child as a reward. We ask you to consider how this perceived "deservedness" aligns with power and privilege. How might play instead serve as *the catalyst* for learning?

Knot 2: Can play be interrupted?

When learners are engaged in play, they are processing their thinking. Processing ideas requires time, space, and a variety of materials. Interrupting rich play interferes with learners' ideas and thought processes. When we shorten time for play abruptly without transition, remove items from learners in play, or intervene in playful pursuits through frequent questioning and comments, we create frustration and stifle the potential for authentic learning. We do need to provoke and sometimes intervene in play, but this should be done in a timely and intentional manner.

Interrupting play is often deeply rooted in the power dynamics that live within our learning spaces. When we interrupt learners in play, we send a blaring message of who is in control and who is not, as well as what tasks should be privileged and what outcomes hold higher value than others. If we see ourselves as co-learners in the space, we need to instead intercede in play in ways that are respectful to the learning process children are engaged in.

Knot 3: Is there a right or wrong way to play?

As educators, we have an obligation to provide caring learning environments that are safe for learners and honor the various forms of play. We must consider learners' developmental competencies as they share what they know through play. The educator's role is to offer intentional opportunities that will evoke richer experiences in play. There is no right or wrong way to play; we provide opportunities for play that guide the pathway for thinking and teaching. As learners interact with their environment, we must consider what they are inviting us to learn about them and how they demonstrate their thinking.

Knot 4: I know learners are more engaged during play, but can play really be assessed?

Play provides the platform for learners to demonstrate their thinking and learning in interconnected and complex ways. When curriculum expectations and standards are foundational to the learning opportunities gifted to children, educators are primed to gain insight into key learning for children. It is important that educators use these optimal conditions to gather information that supports their programming. While play is often referred to as the vehicle for learning, assessment can be viewed as the driver of instruction. Chapter 6 provides more detail about how educators can gather information revealed through play and how this documentation informs next steps in teaching practice.

Knot 5: How can we encourage families, administrators, co-educators, and other colleagues to value play?

We know that partnership is key in supporting learning outcomes for children. Before others can value play, we must first validate the benefits of play for them. Educators must confidently and continuously share how play has benefited their own practice. Welcoming families, administrators, and colleagues into the world of play discourse enhances understanding of curriculum and demonstrates how it is operationalized through play. As educators collect evidence of learning in play settings, they can encourage all stakeholders to collaborate in uncovering the curriculum in these experiences. Assessing documentation over time tells a story of growth that makes learning visible and validates the fundamental reason for supporting play.

Knot 6: Why shift to play-based learning if the results in a traditional approach might appear to be similar?

Play-based approaches to learning offer opportunities for children to move beyond the regurgitation of facts, limited outcomes, and the segregation of subjects. Sustainable thinking that is process oriented allows for problem solving and critical thinking that support an abundance of ideas to merge seamlessly. Play-centric learning environments cultivate the transference of skills and global competencies; they also broaden the scope for assessment to acknowledge different learning styles and support developmental progression.

Knot 7: I know research shows that play benefits learners, but I am afraid of taking the risk and being questioned for this shift in pedagogy.

Play-based learning may be a new concept for many, one that shifts from the expertise of the educator to a co-learning relationship with children and the environment. In this approach, we must relinquish the need to be perfect, rigid, or traditional. Play is a way to support learners' diverse needs, and in keeping with this philosophy of thought, we believe in taking risks to achieve great rewards.

Remember that if we view play as pedagogy, we do not abandon this stance easily. When faced with challenges of implementation, we must see this productive struggle as a learning opportunity; it will command rigor. Once you invite play, you will want it to stay.

Pursuing the Gift

We ask you to consider what steps you will take to pursue the gift of play in your environments for learning. We have highlighted a few suggestions to get you started:

→ **Commit to integrating play as work.** In your program, you may invite children to engage in reading, writing, mathematics, science, and other subjects at different times of the day. Now consider how you can make small shifts to integrate play and interaction into these daily routines. For example, after reading a book, invite learners to engage in a playful opportunity where they use body movement or materials to respond to the text.

→ **Offer choice.** Provide experiences that allow children to demonstrate their thinking in many ways through play. For example, instead of asking children to fill out a graphic organizer only in writing, you can offer them choices to act it out, sketch it out, create music, and more.

→ **Appeal to your learners.** Start with playful experiences that you know children will be interested in. For example, if learners always seem to enjoy musical experiences, consider opportunities where they can use materials to express themselves musically.

Gifts of Learning

As you embark on this journey, we invite you to consider how play can inspire thinking and learning in a variety of ways. To summarize the key concepts explored in this chapter:

→ Play provides avenues for all learners to succeed and is important in developing the social, emotional, biological, and cognitive domains of development.

→ Play is a fundamental right that should be prioritized in learning environments.

→ Play-based learning is foundational to teaching curriculum content.

→ Culturally relevant pedagogy can be adopted to support learners in uncovering their social identities through play while holding high expectations and engaging in critical consciousness.

→ We can deconstruct biases and assumptions through play-centric pedagogy.

As you review these highlights from the chapter, we encourage you to consider these guiding questions as you adapt to a play-centric learning environment:

→ How do you define play?

→ What play experiences were honored or dishonored for you as a child? How has this now influenced your view of and pedagogical approach to play?

→ Where do you see yourself on the continuum of play-based approaches to teaching? What next steps could you take to move toward the center of the continuum?

→ How can you embed culturally relevant pedagogy in your play-based teaching? What are you now considering?

FEATHERS

Phil Cummings   Phil Lesnie

How might these pieces journey with you?

Chapter 2

Creating Spaces That Speak

100 Languages

No way. The hundred is there.
The child
is made of one hundred.
The child has
a hundred languages
a hundred hands
a hundred thoughts
a hundred ways of thinking
of playing, of speaking.
A hundred always a hundred
ways of listening
of marveling of loving
a hundred joys
for singing and understanding
a hundred worlds
to discover
a hundred worlds
to invent
a hundred worlds
to dream.
The child has
a hundred languages
(and a hundred hundred hundred more)
but they steal ninety-nine.

The school and the culture
separate the head from the body.
They tell the child:
to think without hands
to do without head
to listen and not to speak
to understand without joy
to love and to marvel
only at Easter and Christmas.
They tell the child:
to discover the world already there
and of the hundred
they steal ninety-nine.
They tell the child:
that work and play
reality and fantasy
science and imagination
sky and earth
reason and dream
are things
that do not belong together.
And thus they tell the child
that the hundred is not there.
The child says:
No way. The hundred is there.

–Loris Malaguzzi
(translated by Lella Gandini)

The "One Hundred Languages" is a metaphor for the extraordinary potentials of children, their knowledge-building and creative processes, the myriad forms with which life is manifested and knowledge is constructed. The hundred languages are understood as having the potential to be transformed and multiplied in the cooperation and interaction between the languages, among the children, and between children and adults. (Rinaldi 2013)

An environment that fosters the one hundred languages will gift learners with all the pleasures the world has to offer. In spaces that invite joy, we witness the marvels experienced by our senses and see the contributions of each child valued and held in high esteem. These spaces speak to wonders, discoveries, and delightful pursuits that connect our memories.

Mapping Memories

Our memories have the power to inform our perceptions, shape our trajectories, and influence our beliefs. Consider a favorite childhood memory involving play, and reflect on the following questions:

→ What kind of play brought you joy and helped you learn about yourself and the people and places around you?

→ How might time have played a role in this experience?

→ What materials did you enjoy playing with most?

→ Where were you?

→ Who was with you?

→ How did this memory make you feel?

When we draw close to the narratives of childhood memories, we may envision joyful moments fostered by limitless time in the outdoors, imaginative play, risk taking, creative use of materials, and the development of relationships with others (Curtis and Carter 2015). The "one hundred languages" we spoke as children live within the memories we cherish in our hearts. Through play, our languages enhanced the ways in which we were able to make sense of the world, demonstrate our thinking, and share our diverse competencies. Memories help children develop neurological pathways in the brain for future learning and the maturation of capabilities (Curtis and Jaboneta 2019). Play-based environments that offer differentiated opportunities encourage such memories and invite learners to command a space where play flourishes to foster choice and voice.

The more often you share what you've learned, the stronger that information will become in your memory.

—Steve Brunkhorst

In considering your own learning environments and curriculum programming, how might you offer opportunities for children to create experiences that evolve into everlasting memories? When we think about the opportunities we gift to our learners, we must consider whether our spaces speak to the languages that best allow children to represent their thinking in ways that honor their multiple identities and lived experiences. Do our spaces allow the one hundred languages to resound loudly, or do they center only the desires and interests of the educator? We invite you to think back to your prior learning environments:

→ Which of the one hundred languages were honored for you as a child?

→ Which languages were dishonored?

→ Which languages can you offer in your own learning environment now as an educator?

The concept of the one hundred languages compels us to merge learners' interests, competencies, and desires in the learning environments we establish.

> Spaces are typically created with some kind of purpose or intention, whether or not this is evident. Every environment implies a set of values or beliefs about the people who use a space and the activities that take place there. (Curtis and Carter 2015, 19)

The Environment Is a Teacher

The environment serves as a gift that encourages children to engage in their learning spaces with intention. The learning environment should be an organic space that is ever changing and evolving. As educators gather insight from learners, families, and the community, they should adjust the learning space to respond to and reflect those needs. There has been a shift away from designing spaces simply for decorative and aesthetic purposes. When establishing a learning environment, thoughts and intention must be centered around a space for thinking and learning.

Lella Gandini, world-renowned educator and U.S. liaison for dissemination of the Reggio Emilia Approach, notes that "the environment is the most visible aspect of the work done in the schools by all the protagonists. It conveys the message that this is a place where adults have thought about the quality and instructive power of space" (as cited in Carter 2007, 23). The families, learners, and educators together are the protagonists. The enchanted nature of a learning space stems from the influential power and agency of the protagonists.

We believe that families, learners, and educators serve as provocateurs who each play an interdependent role in building sustainable climates where thinking and learning thrive (see figure 2.1). The collaboration between the learning environment and the provocateurs invites opportunities for response, clarification, and expansion. The atmosphere in which children grow should be founded on co-construction. This approach asks educators to be open to the vulnerability of not being the sole holder of power. Co-construction of the learning environment also honors learners' Rights to Spaces (discussed in more detail later in the chapter). Partnerships are transformed through a collaborative process that is not driven singularly by our own beliefs, ideas, and inputs. When we make these decisions without the investment of the protagonists, we deny opportunities for deeper engagement and intentionality. Having the ability and power to make choices is a privilege.

→ Who has the power to honor or dishonor the rights within a space?

→ Who do we position as being the holder of such rights?

Figure 2.1. Protagonists Who Inform the Learning Environment

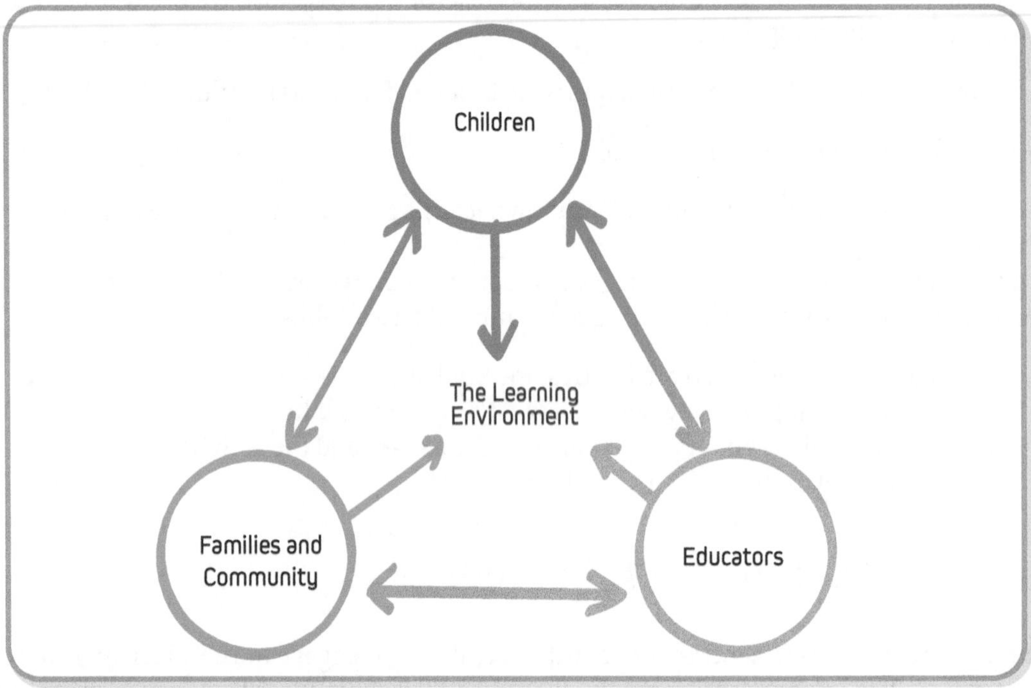

Karyn Callaghan gives insight into how to think about the environment:

> As educators we need to increasingly move away from thinking
> of ourselves as disseminators of knowledge to being provocateurs,
> documenters, and meaning-makers, alongside the other protagonists.
> As we reflect on our beliefs about children, we must consider
> our role in supporting the environment. Many believe that the
> environment *is* a teacher. As children navigate their thinking, they
> read the environment that is gifted to them. When we as educators
> can interpret the many layers of learners' interactions within an
> environment, this becomes an asset to our work. (Callaghan 2013, 1)

Elements of the Learning Environment

In the early years, the learning environment includes not only the classroom's physical indoor space but also the outdoors—creating an atmosphere that offers elements of physical space, time, materials, and relationships. These four elements function interdependently to support learning and thinking aligned with the curriculum. Physical arrangements of a space often inform the time learners spend with the materials offered and reflect the relationships that they build as a community. As noted in our discussion of culturally relevant pedagogy in chapter 1, we want to communicate values that hold true to the cultural competence, critical consciousness, and high expectations co-constructed by the protagonists of the space.

We must establish atmospheres that create and sustain foundations for learning that are responsive and extensive and that challenge learners to reach their fullest potential. Every change a child or an educator makes in a learning environment might lead to an intentional shift of the elements in a space. Thoughts and ideas are followed by actions that shift and transform the learning community anew, and an iterative journey begins to take shape.

The following section explores the four elements of physical space, time, materials, and relationships in connection with these considerations for learning environments:

- → Flexibility
- → Extension of the space
- → Intention
- → Co-construction
- → Variety
- → Sensory experience
- → Child-centered focus

Physical Space

Learning environments for young children should be arranged with attention to elements of aesthetics, flexibility, invitation, safety, nurture, and function. We refer to the learning space itself as a teacher because it cultivates and influences the learning. As children seek ownership in a space, their interests, curiosities, wonders, and tensions for learning deepen (Felstiner 2004). Children require physical spaces that satisfy their desires to explore, question, manipulate, and share their stories. Before welcoming children into a community, we need to carefully consider how the physical space will provide multiple opportunities for learners to interact with the educator, their peers, the materials, and time.

When we plan physical environments with these considerations in mind, we use intention in implementing items in the learning space, as well as in repositioning, modifying, or removing items. We are cognizant of how a physical space that is thoughtfully designed for learning will invite all protagonists to think, explore, and interact with intention.

We encourage you to consider the following when designing a physical space:

Consideration and Connection to Physical Space	Examples
Flexibility Ensure that the space can be transformed in open-ended ways. Shift furniture and change configurations within the space based on learners' interactions in the environment.	A few learners are seen bumping their legs as they squeeze through the space between a unit shelf and a table that are too close together. The educator responds by moving this table to allow for more freedom of movement in the space.
Extension of the space Design and construct learning spaces in the outdoor environment that might reflect, respond to, or extend experiences children have indoors. Ensure that the learning environment goes beyond the walls to extend to the hallways, outdoors, and community.	The educator places a large chalkboard outdoors, hangs materials intentionally on the fence nearby, and arranges little cushions in a circle on the grass.
Intention Establish spaces that intentionally center children's wonders, curiosities, and intelligences. If learners are drawn to a learning opportunity that generates more interest than the space allows for, consider shifting the opportunity to a larger space or establishing another area that might speak similarly to children's needs and interests.	An educator notices that learners crowding around a small table are captivated by the shimmer of jewels, glass beads, crystals, and mirrors offered. The next day, the educator rearranges the experience in a larger space by a window, where learners will be able to observe light refracting to create rainbows and shadows on the wall.

(Continued)

Consideration and Connection to Physical Space	Examples
Co-construction Invite learners to share ideas about the learning environment. When a learning opportunity is offered within the space, gather insight and ideas from learners on the possibilities for location and positioning.	The educator and learners draw a map together to show where they would like learning opportunities to be placed within the space. They have discussions about their ideas and how they might be implemented.
Variety Provide varied spaces within the classroom that reflect learners' preferences for engagement. Offer and create places at various levels, heights, perspectives, and angles. Provide spaces where children have opportunities to stand, lie on their tummies, have aerial views, or lie on their backs, both indoors and outdoors.	The educator designs a learning space that offers beanbag seating, high tables for engaging while standing, wooden stump seating, cozy couches, and more.
Sensory experience Invite opportunities for learners' senses to be engaged within the space. Establish areas where learners can congregate and engage in play that requires space, while accounting for the level of sound, sensory opportunities, lighting, and various textures. Consider muting the classroom walls with neutral tones to create a sense of calm.	Learners are intrigued by the way light creates shadows in the space; the educator then responds by shifting the furniture to invite a large space for shadow play that builds on these emerging curiosities. On a colorful bulletin board, the educator has posted a collection of photos that reflect a playful experience highlighting learning from weeks prior. The educator realizes that learners are not attending to the learning on this board and decides to remove the colorful background to bring attention to the documentation. Once the background is neutralized, the photos are highlighted and more accessible to learners.
Child-centered focus Ensure that the furniture is age-appropriate and that children can easily access resources and materials in the space. Establish prime learning areas that are not consumed by adult materials.	The educator kneels down and scans the room to view it from the learners' perspective and repositions furniture and materials to ensure accessibility. The educator also realizes that their desk is positioned on a carpeted area that could be used for more large-group engagement, so they decide to remove the desk from this prime learning area.

Time

Learning is timeless. When we invite children into a world of play, we aim to capture moments of engagement that sustain learning and thinking over time. A space that honors time invites the educator to process information in a way that considers learners' needs, interests, and schemas. The element of time offers possibilities for development, growth, and learning. When time is used effectively, children can establish relationships with the materials, make logical connections to the flow of the day, and reimagine how to navigate the space.

The time spent in the learning environment sets the foundation for the day and week. When educators plan and organize their time, they deliver focused instruction with precision. What we offer in a day should be communicated in collaboration with children to ensure the engagement of all protagonists. Here are some considerations for time in your learning space:

Consideration and Connection to Time	Examples
Flexibility Ensure that the day remains open to change, flexibility, and reimagination.	The educator recognizes that learners appear tired in the afternoon before independent reading time. The educator makes changes to the schedule to allow for body movement time.
Extension of the space Offer large blocks of uninterrupted play-based learning indoors, outdoors, and in the community.	The educator explicitly plans time for engaging in the outdoor classroom beyond recess and lunch breaks, such as community walks, intentional whole-group instruction in the outdoor classroom that connects to play, and conducting a read-aloud.
Intention Plan a flow of the day that offers learning in large groups, small groups, and individual settings to maximize learning throughout the day. Adopt a three-part pedagogy that highlights instructional needs, student interests, and curriculum expectations.	The educator acknowledges that there are many subject areas to cover and purposefully plans for the day and week, ensuring that lessons are cross-curricular (see the section on the flow of the day later in the chapter).
Co-construction Ensure that time and scheduling are communicated to and co-constructed with learners.	The weather forecast predicts thunderstorms in the afternoon, so the educator seeks learners' opinions on how to honor outdoor classroom time in light of the forecast.
Variety Offer varied experiences for instruction and engagement throughout the day where learners can engage with time in a variety of ways.	The educator allows time for instruction and for movement, collaboration, and play. The educator designs time to meet with learners in large groups, small groups, and independent learning experiences.
Sensory experience Infuse sensory opportunities into transitional times and throughout the day (e.g., recess, lunch, preparation time, cleanup).	When the educator is transitioning from one area or space to another, they engage in singing, call and response, or movement. During independent reading time, the educator plays calming music to promote a relaxing and enjoyable atmosphere.
Child-centered focus Create shifts in time to accommodate learners' needs, strengths, and interests. Allocate time based on learners' developmental needs to account for large blocks of play and required minutes of literacy and numeracy instruction.	During outdoor play, learners are most curious about the seasonal changes they have observed. The educator recognizes that the children need more time to make connections in the outdoors and extends the outdoor time in response.

Materials

In an intentionally designed space, playful pieces are carefully arranged to bring meaning to a child. The educator organizes, presents, and uses materials to promote deep learning and engagement. The materials offered in the learning environment should be open-ended and offered in ways that highlight many possibilities for children to use them. We encourage you to consider these things when choosing materials for your learning space:

Consideration and Connection to Materials	Examples
Flexibility Provide open-ended materials that encourage choice and flexibility. Empower children to use the materials fluidly within various spaces.	A child uses fabric to represent the landscape in a story, then uses the same fabric to create clothing for a wooden peg person in another learning space.
Extension of the space Allow children opportunities to collect open-ended materials from the outdoors, then offer these materials in the indoor learning environment (while conversely offering indoor materials in the outdoors).	In the indoor learning space, the educator presents a flower or a nest found outdoors to extend learning. The educator shifts a learning opportunity with open-ended materials offered indoors to a location outside.
Intention Intentionally provide a variety of open-ended materials that connect to schematic play, culture, and curriculum.	The educator notices that a learner is spinning different materials in the classroom. In response, the educator then offers bangles that are relevant to the child's culture and that can be spun during play that aligns with a learning opportunity focused on curriculum.
Co-construction Invite families to share materials found within the home or community that can be used for many possibilities in play.	The educator sends a letter home that welcomes contributions of found objects that can be used in open-ended ways in the classroom.
Variety Consider the availability, accessibility, quantity, and arrangement of the materials to allow for engagement in the environment.	The educator decides to present materials of different shapes, sizes, and colors in various areas of the learning environment.
Sensory experience Offer a variety of colors, sounds, and textures that appeal to a variety of senses.	The educator offers open-ended materials, such as blocks with colorful water inside, metal pieces that create sounds, fabric with various textures, and more.
Child-centered focus Offer materials that reflect children's wonderings, ideas, passions, interests, theories, and prior knowledge. Understand learners in the space, and consider their ages, safety, and specific needs when choosing materials.	The educator notices that many children enjoy stroking smooth objects. The educator then offers cowrie shells in the environment to meet learners' sensory needs and connect to their Caribbean heritage. The educator offers a variety of materials in the learning environment that can be easily washed or sanitized to ensure learners' safety.

Relationships

Our sense of belonging results from the dialogues, social exchanges, and interactions that set the stage for learning conditions. The relationships cultivated in the learning environment are essential to fostering learners' connections with peers, educators, materials, and the physical space. Educators should spend time scaffolding how to build these connections to the elements of the learning space:

Consideration and Connection to Relationships	Examples
Flexibility Ensure that the elements in the learning environment are ever changing and never static. Create an environment that allows for choice and for the protagonists to interact with materials, physical space, and time.	In a learning community, children are able to choose which spaces they interact with, which materials they use, and which peers they collaborate with, and they can represent their thinking in a variety of ways. There are spaces where learners can design and build, while other spaces allow for artistic expression and writing, invite storytelling, or build on scientific inquiries.
Extension of the space Extend the learning environment outdoors to seamlessly build on the relationships made indoors.	On a community walk, learners discover a branch with buds from a tree near the window. The educator honors the children's intrigue by offering the branch in close proximity to the window, along with a magnifying glass, for the children to make deeper connections. The educator and school librarian develop a partnership where they co-plan and co-create learning opportunities that will be offered in the library to support texts read in both that space and the classroom.
Intention Create spaces that encourage connections, collaboration, and a sense of belonging.	In the learning space, learners have used blocks to represent the Taj Mahal and other buildings they have observed in their travels. The educator considers how to build on these ideas, seeking pictures and books from families and other community members.
Co-construction Offer materials within the learning space that make home–school connections (e.g., photos, cultural artifacts). Welcome families and community members into the classroom to co-teach with the educator.	Learners have shown interest in picture books that share refugee stories. The educator welcomes families and a local community group that advocates for immigrant justice into the classroom to share stories and deepen understanding around this topic.

(Continued)

Consideration and Connection to Relationships	Examples
Variety Foster a variety of relationships that will provoke different perspectives and points of view. Layer a variety of materials over time so that learners can develop new relationships with the materials.	A child is observed making new connections to a classmate after the classmate's mother shares a recipe for making roti. The children are now comparing the different breads they make at home, such as naan and bannock. The educator responds to the children's interests by placing natural wood slices in an area that offers wooden peg people and providing a book to provoke their thinking (*Bread, Bread, Bread* by Ann Morris).
Sensory experience Create and build a sense of place where learners see, hear, and feel connected to one another.	The children and educators in a space commit to ongoing knowledge building and community circles where everyone has opportunities to share ideas, wonderings, challenges, and feelings in a supportive and collaborative way.
Child-centered focus Provide opportunities for learners, families, and communities to be invested in the learning environment through cultural practices, perspective, and vision.	Families have been invited to engage in an outdoor walk with learners to collect materials that will be offered in the classroom. Families and learners then use the collection of materials to demonstrate ideas connected to a book the learners have enjoyed reading in class.

See the next page for a template you can use to scan your own learning space to determine whether it takes into account the considerations for learning environments, as well as what next steps you can take to make the space meet these goals. This template is also provided in the Digital Resources (see page 219).

Template for Scanning Your Learning Space

Consideration	Observations/Notes/Next Steps	
Flexibility Spaces should allow for choice and interaction among protagonists (learners, educators, families, community members), materials, physical space, and time. The elements should be ever changing and never static.		
Extension of the space The learning environment should go beyond the classroom walls to extend to the hallways, outdoors, and community.		
Intention Spaces should be established with intention and a focus on strengths, needs, and interests that center wonder, curiosity, and intellectual rigor.		
Co-construction Learners should be invited to share ideas about the learning environment.		
Variety Varied spaces should be provided within the classroom to ensure that the environment considers learners' preferences for engagement. Learning opportunities should be placed at various levels, heights, perspectives, and angles.		
Sensory experience Opportunities should be offered where learners' senses can be engaged within the space. Areas should be established for learners to congregate and engage in play that requires space, while accounting for levels of sound, sensory opportunities, lighting, and various textures.		
Child-centered focus Furniture should be age-appropriate so that children can access resources and materials in the space easily. Prime learning areas should not be consumed by adult materials.		

Disrupting Spaces That Silence

Our learning spaces often are mirrors of our own beliefs and values. Without conversation or explanation, environments speak loudly to what the educator and learners value and deem important. The privileges and power afforded through the design of a space send explicit and implicit messages to learners and their families about what is prioritized and what is not. Spaces may speak loudly to our assumptions and biases but may speak softly to the authentic realities of learners in the environment.

Our notion of the learning environment shifts when we consider it as a "living space" personalized by the stories and events of the learners who inhabit it (Felstiner 2004). Our educational experiences can condition us to replicate legacies of the past, challenge the status quo, or overcome the void of experiences we might have not been afforded ourselves. In every space, we engage in power dynamics that grant learners access to succeed or deny opportunity for learners to thrive. Power imbalances result when educators adapt the destructive mindsets that too often permeate our learning environments and create spaces that speak to inequity.

In a moving keynote address at an International Literacy Association Intensive in Nevada, Cornelius Minor (2019) spoke to these destructive mindsets, which stem from implicit beliefs that shape our pedagogical practice. These mindsets uphold notions of inequality and create barriers to equitable approaches for teaching. They can take the form of the following ideas within the learning space:

1. **Deservedness:** the implicit belief that the educator will agree to deliver sound programming *if* learners demonstrate that they have earned it. For example, an educator offers a space where learners can engage in design and engineering with a variety of materials. Children are observed using the materials in unconventional ways. The educator immediately removes all the materials and comments to another educator, "They won't get these materials back because they are not showing that they deserve them."

2. **"Should-know" mentality:** the assumption of what a child *should* know and the cultural capital they *should* carry. For example, an educator designs a space to invite artistic expression by placing a variety of materials for learners to use, including markers, crayons, paints, and paintbrushes. Children are observed dipping paintbrushes already coated with one color into a paint pod of a different color, which results in the paint being mixed. The educator scolds the learners by saying, "You are mixing everything! You should know how to use the paints properly."

3. **Forced gratitude:** the notion that an educator's acts of kindness and their investment in the learning are contingent on learners' appreciation of the investment. For example, the educator presents beautiful offerings in the learning environment and says, "I hope you are very thankful for what I have offered here. Make sure you use this with care; not many spaces have this."

While many of us have adopted these destructive mindsets from time to time, we must remember how this mode of thinking is rooted in notions of power and privilege. With such mindsets, the educator assumes a position of power and asserts it upon learners in ways that create a superiority complex where what the educator values is deemed most important, denying the experiences, voices, and opinions of the learners. Destructive mindsets affect how learners engage, respond, and interact with the environment.

We all hold implicit biases, which are defined as attitudes or stereotypes that affect our understanding, actions, and decisions in an unconscious manner (Kirwan Institute, as cited in Friedman and Mwenelupembe 2020). These biases can affect children's well-being, as well as their thinking, so as educators, we must engage in a continuous cycle of learning and unlearning. To establish culturally relevant and responsive learning environments, we must understand our own identities, the biases we hold, and how our biases affect learners. While we might not intend to express implicit biases, our learning spaces share multiple messages that learners unconsciously absorb; they measure their own identities against what is standardized within the space. "What children do not see in the classroom teaches children as much as what they do see" (Derman-Sparks and Edwards 2010, 43).

Envision each child in your classroom; move through your learning space and consider their perspectives:

→ How are learners' social identities reflected in this space?

→ How can you honor and explore their families' ideas, questions, and identities?

→ How can you value social identities that are not visible (e.g., class, sexual orientation) within the environment?

→ How can you explore identities and aspects of culture beyond foods, festivals, and clothing? What might our intentions be when offering these particular aspects of culture?

→ What shifts can you make within your space?

The freedoms we offer in our learning spaces humanize children and liberate them from any "threats to their identities, cultural values, and know-how" (Shalaby 2017, xv). We have a responsibility to create spaces that honor learners' rights and create equitable spaces for all children.

Rights to Spaces

Imagine a space where children have the autonomy to navigate a learning environment that fulfills their individual rights—a space that calls on their expressions, capabilities, and intelligences. Children have rights that must be upheld and centered in the spaces we design. Such learning environments require the commitment of educators who share a vision for the design of the space. In chapter 1, we discussed play as a right, and we therefore encourage you to consider what rights our learning environments serve for the children who live and learn within them. A space that does not foster these rights will render the child silent and nurture a culture of compliance or chaos. Spaces speak to the values we hold and the future memories learners will create. The following pages show the rights we must speak to within our spaces (adapted from Curtis and Carter 2015).

1. Children must be allowed creativity in expressing their knowledge through a variety of open-ended materials that honor divergent thinking and ways of knowing (see figures 2.2a, b, c).

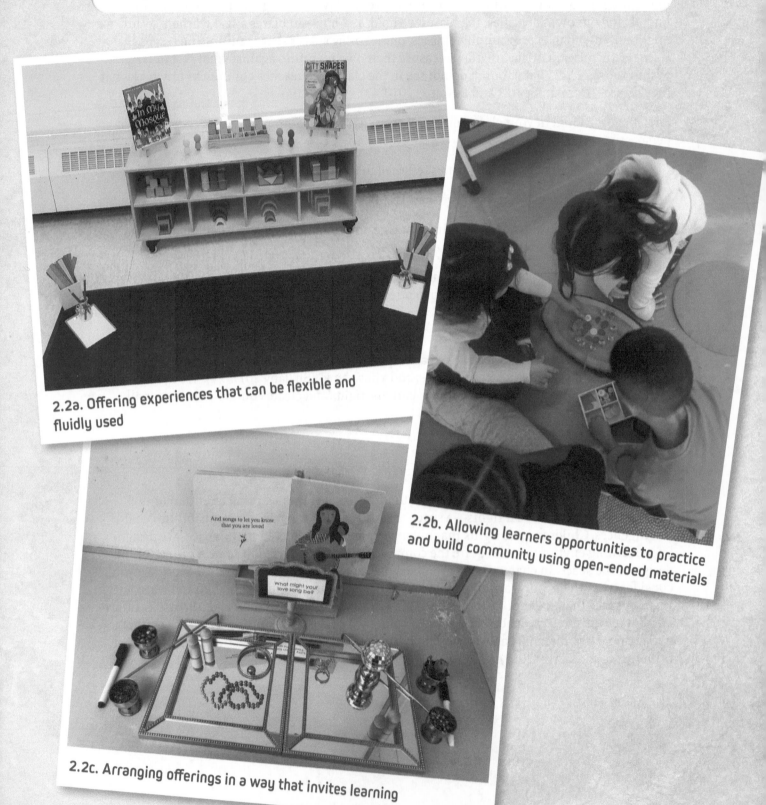

2.2a. Offering experiences that can be flexible and fluidly used

2.2b. Allowing learners opportunities to practice and build community using open-ended materials

2.2c. Arranging offerings in a way that invites learning

2. We must affirm children's ideas as they use open-ended materials to express their thinking (see figure 2.3).

2.3. Learners manipulating materials in different ways to show their thinking around what it means to be in community

3. Children learn best when offered interesting materials, ample time, and opportunity to investigate, transform, and invent (see figures 2.4a, b).

2.4a. Making use of the changes within the natural environment to capitalize on learners' ideas about the world

2.4b. Offering opportunities for learners to tinker and explore materials and their functionality

4. Children have vivid imaginations and theories about the world, which need to be explored over a period of time (see figure 2.5, where the question, image, book, or other open-ended materials are added to and removed from learning experiences to extend learners' thinking).

2.5. Presenting materials over time in different ways that invite new learning

5. Children need multiple ways to build a solid identity and connections with those around them—their families, peers, role models, culture, and community, as well as the natural world (see figures 2.6a, b).

2.6a. Building an environment that allows learners to express how they see themselves and their families

2.6b. Learners celebrating and sharing how they see themselves with their families

6. Children have active bodies and a desire for adventure; they have the right to show adults how powerful and competent they are (see figures 2.7a, b).

2.7a. Children sharing their stories and ideas about skin color in an active way

2.7b. Children building relationships with the outdoors through investigation and exploration

7. Children need to have a sense of ownership within the learning space through routines and opportunities that promote community (see figures 2.8a, b).

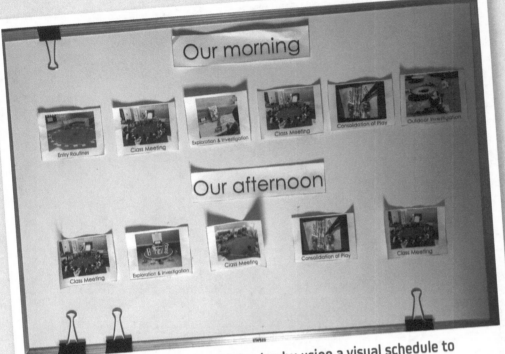

2.8a. Co-constructing the flow of the day by using a visual schedule to respond to emerging needs

2.8b. Gathering as a community to discuss the learning conditions for the classroom, using an inquiry stance

8. Children deserve to be surrounded by beauty, softness, and comfort, as well as order and attention to health and safety (see figures 2.9a, b).

2.9a. Presenting learning at different levels within the classroom space that offer intrigue, allure, and softness

2.9b. Providing learners with opportunities to self-regulate their needs

In honoring these Rights to Spaces, we center learners' voices, experiences, and gifts. By upholding these rights, we move away from perpetuating cycles of inheritance that limit learners' potential and thinking in the learning environment. As learners live within our spaces, they offer invitations that we as educators accept or deny on a daily basis. We must design and craft spaces that honor the dignity of learners' curiosities and intelligences. Sometimes when we are faced with challenges in our learning spaces, we mistakenly think that learners—rather than the learning environment—need to change. But in our own learning journey, our greatest lessons have come from children who challenged our thinking and invited us to reenvision our practice in pedagogically responsive and transformative ways. These children inspired us to shift how we offered teaching and learning in our spaces.

The children we speak of are often pathologized, dehumanized, and identified as troublemakers. In our experience, these are learners who speak loudly (verbally or nonverbally) or in emotional ways when their rights are denied in the learning space. Carla Shalaby (2017) sees these so-called troublemakers as canaries caged in a toxic classroom environment. Historically, canaries were used to alert miners to dangerous conditions in the mines. If toxic gases were present, the canaries would react first, signaling the miners to exit immediately. Similarly, children send signals to warn educators of the harms and threats that surface in the learning environment. Their misbehavior should be seen as an invitation for us to question, investigate, and reflect on our practices and what messages we communicate through the learning space.

When children raise their voices in search of acknowledgment and visibility, we should respond by shifting the learning environment to foster a space where children are free to learn and grow (Shalaby 2017). Our responsibility as educators is to transform our learning environments to reshape power and hierarchical structures that privilege authority; we must think about whether the learning environment has prepared each learner for success or failure.

Designing Spaces

Imagine that it is the end of your summer vacation, and a new school year is about to start. Whether it is your first or thirty-first year of teaching, a mix of emotions floods your senses, and you are now faced with the task of designing a space. You might be negotiating several challenges: limited time for classroom setup, minimal resources or furniture, or new administrators with visions that have shifted. Yet at the heart of it all, your design needs to center the learners. Your learning environment should foster collaboration, communication, problem solving, and innovation to create a sense of community.

We invest in our environment when we merge the one hundred languages referred to by Loris Malaguzzi (2011) in seamless ways through the four elements of time, physical space, materials, and relationships. Spaces speak to the competencies of our languages as much as they speak to learners' growth and needs. If we design a space that presents learning in subject-specific ways, we deliver messages that do not make connections through a multidisciplinary approach. By avoiding a siloed approach to the learning environment, we bolster the capabilities of children who benefit from making connections to literacy, math, science, art, music, physical education, and more. This approach allows the environment to foster a community of learning that surpasses a regurgitation of facts and enables learners to think in interdisciplinary ways.

As you design spaces for learning, we encourage you to think about how children will engage with their learning environment. Student engagement drives our intention in designing a space that speaks to learners. We invite learners to interact with the space in ways that provoke the one hundred languages. Learning spaces should speak to the following:

Self-regulation: Spaces should speak to learners having choice and voice. Educators can provide learners with opportunities for self-regulated snacks (brought from home or provided by the school), rest, or calm (see figures 2.10a, b, c).

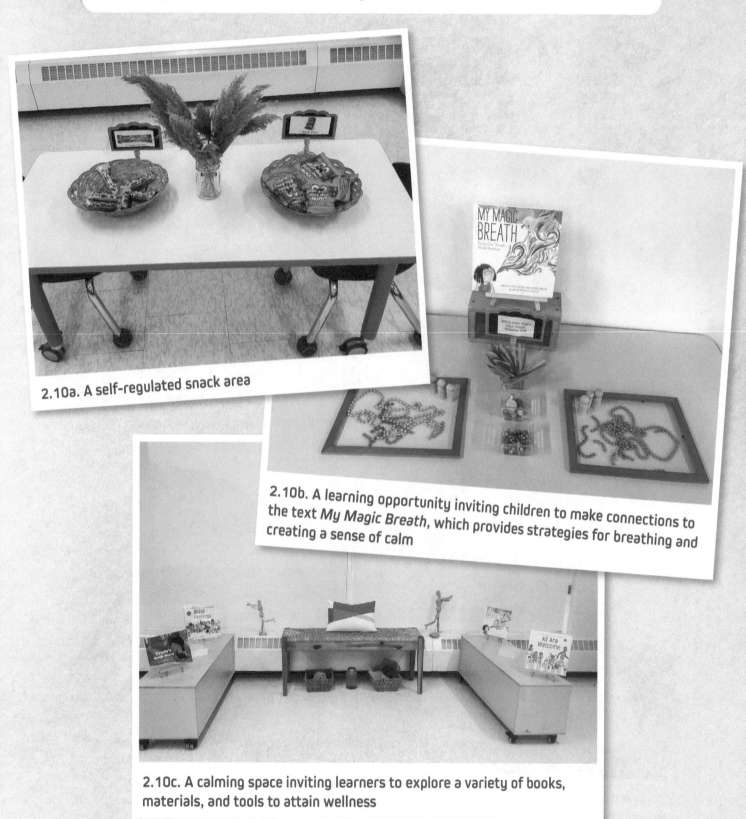

2.10a. A self-regulated snack area

2.10b. A learning opportunity inviting children to make connections to the text *My Magic Breath*, which provides strategies for breathing and creating a sense of calm

2.10c. A calming space inviting learners to explore a variety of books, materials, and tools to attain wellness

Art expression: Spaces should invite learners to express themselves artistically through dramatic play, visual arts, and music (see figures 2.11a, b).

2.11a. Shelving with a variety of art materials to inspire learners' artistic creations

2.11b. A palette of watercolors, a bouquet of flowers, and materials placed on small canvases to welcome artistic creation

Natural curiosity: Spaces should connect to nature's wonders, discoveries, and phenomena (see figures 2.12a, b, c).

2.12a. A learning opportunity fostering inquiry, curiosity, and exploration through open-ended materials found in the outdoors that support the text *We All Play*

2.12b. A learning opportunity offering the book *Festival of Colors* along with a variety of materials for exploring artistic expression through nature

2.12c. A learning opportunity offering the book *Feathers* along with materials for exploring the gifts of nature

Design and engineering: Spaces should allow children to engage in problem solving and innovation (see figures 2.13a, b, c, d).

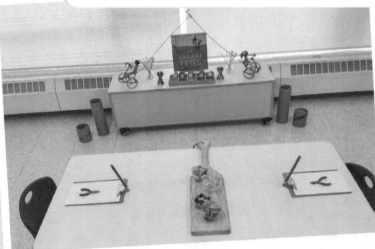

2.13a. A space that honors learners' creativity and innovative visions by offering tools, open-ended materials, simple machines, and the book *Jabari Tries* to inspire design within the learning environment

2.13b. An unplugged coding experience inviting children to use the materials offered to respond to the book *Where Are You From?*

2.13c. Offering a variety of materials that support building and design, paired with the books *Boxitects* and *Dreaming Up* to encourage problem solving and innovation

2.13d. A learning opportunity showcasing the book *Be a Maker* and wire figures to spark curiosity, with open-ended materials to encourage design thinking

Sensory engagement: Spaces should provoke learners to connect with their senses to spark discovery, promote engagement, meet sensory needs, and find joy (see figures 2.14a, b, c).

2.14a. Wooden blocks paired with a light table to invite intrigue and allow learners to make connections to the book *This Is Ruby*

2.14b. Possibilities for play with sand inspired by the book *Rocket Says Clean Up!*

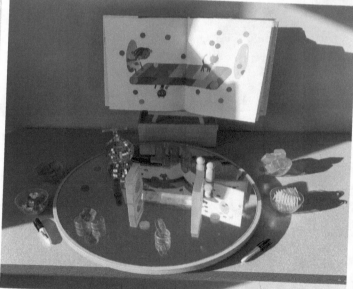

2.14c. The book *Another* paired with materials intentionally placed where the natural light creates opportunity for shadow play and reflection

Symbolic representation: Spaces should present opportunities for children to interact in symbolic representations that support literacy and mathematical behaviors (see figures 2.15a, b, c).

2.15a. The books *In My Mosque* and *City Shapes* paired with colored blocks, clipboards with paper, pencils, and peg people to invite opportunities for symbolic representation

2.15b. Welcoming learners to communicate messages of encouragement in relation to the text *The Invisible Boy*

2.15c. Providing opportunities to make connections to the book *In My Mosque* through playful pieces

Places of belonging: Spaces should foster inclusivity and diversity and welcome learners' lived experiences (see figures 2.16a, b).

2.16a. A space intentionally designed to celebrate diversity by offering a variety of books and art supplies

2.16b. A family tree placed in the learning environment to foster a sense of belonging and contribution

Designing spaces with intention requires great attention to learners' habits, behaviors, attitudes, and values. We design spaces to access prior knowledge, extend thinking, and respond to challenges that present themselves in teaching. A space should function for learners; it should be authentic to living and learning while allowing for the creation of lasting memories. We offer these carefully designed spaces as gifts to children; when they enter such a space, they unwrap the gift, and a revelatory process of learning ensues.

Living within Spaces That Speak

Living within a learning environment requires that we know how much time is available to us and how we will make use of it. Spaces that honor play-based learning affirm that the use of time is essential for effectively planning our days and offering comprehensive approaches to teaching. In such environments, we deliberately devise a *flow of the day* that considers the use of time and space to maximize children's learning.

The flow of the day should be flexible and fluid and transferred in different learning contexts with minimal transitions. The ebb and flow of the day are responsive to learners' needs, interests, and wants. The flow of the day is adaptable and makes more authentic connections to children, as the plan is co-constructed to maximize learning across the curriculum (Ontario Ministry of Education 2016b, 95).

Time waits for no one; it is nonrenewable and is the one thing we can never get back. When you reflect on your days with learners, ask yourself these questions:

→ How should your time be spent within the environment?

→ What can you offer in the time you are gifted with learners?

→ How are learners' interests, curiosities, and wonders considered within the flow of the day?

When co-constructing your flow of the day, we invite you to include the following:

→ Large *uninterrupted* blocks of time in the indoor and outdoor classroom dedicated to play and inquiry-based learning that aligns with curriculum expectations

→ Whole-group instruction that is *focused* and *concise*

→ Small-group and/or independent instruction to address learners' particular *needs* and *interests* (e.g., small-group reading opportunities, scaffolding loose parts)

→ Opportunities for self-regulated rest, snacks, and exploration throughout the day

→ Schedules *co-constructed* with learners to allow for fluidity and flow

→ A *visual schedule* that is accessible and shares the sequenced events of the day

Two sample flow-of-the-day schedules (including one with visuals) are presented in the Digital Resources (see page 219).

Shifting Spaces

Envision your learning space as a living thing that grows, evolves, and changes over time. Much like a plant, it adapts and transforms continuously as the environment nourishes its needs. When changes are made to the environment, certainties become questions and new ideas are brought to life. Our learning environments are not static; they are flexible, fluid, and ever changing. Transformation is inevitable when we allow learners to lead us.

> When a flower doesn't bloom, you fix the environment in which it grows, not the flower.
> —Alexander Den

As you consider the moves that you will make in your learning environment, we encourage you to think about shifting legacies you have inherited, your mindsets, your practices, and your pedagogy.

Instead of doing this:	Shift to doing this:
Offering spaces that are subject- or theme-specific and that only isolate learning goals	Allowing subject areas to be integrated and observed throughout the learning space
Taking a static, adult-driven perspective of the learning space	Presenting learning in a way that can be transformed, reinvented, and co-constructed
Designing a space solely based on decorations and adornments	Designing a space with intention to highlight learners' work and theories
Designing a space that overstimulates learners with color, sound, and visual clutter	Designing an environment that offers a sense of calm through muted tones, carefully selected materials, and warm and inviting spaces
Using time in an adult-directed way that does not consider learners' needs as they navigate time, space, materials, and relationships	Using time in a student-centered way that invites all elements of space to be understood with responsiveness
Celebrating culture in tokenistic and misappropriated ways	Honoring learners' lived experiences, cultures, and social identities in authentic ways that are infused seamlessly
Being inflexible about where learning happens (e.g., teaching only within the indoor classroom space)	Leveraging multiple spaces for learning opportunities beyond the indoors (e.g., the community, the library, the hallways, the outdoors)

Our spaces should create conditions that optimize learning and respond to what protagonists reveal to us. Our spaces are dynamic and are subject to change. As you consider the shifts you need to make in your practice, we invite you to envision a space that is *brave, bold,* and *beautiful.*

Additional Considerations

Missed Invitations

When we present a space for children to learn and think, we make observations that reinform how we construct the environment. We have explored ideas that center our spaces as fluid, flexible, and ever changing. As we make shifts to our environment, we test our theories and invite new possibilities. And because insights do not always reveal themselves immediately and are sometimes made clear in hindsight, we must retrace our path by taking up the opportunities we have missed or the misconceptions that can arise:

Missed Invitation 1: Spaces do not require collaboration.

We invite you to question who the space is for and what purpose it serves. Our spaces should be collaborative communities that honor multiple voices and divergent and creative thinking. When we aim to collaborate with protagonists, they too become investors in the space, and the returns are greater as they take ownership of the space that is in service to them. When the learning environment is driven by the educator, the decisions, choices, and offerings serve only the educator's agenda, which may be traditionally inherited.

Missed Invitation 2: Spaces require a theme-based approach.

The design of a learning space should focus on the intention of the learning, not the decor. When the decor itself becomes the focus, the entire learning space assumes the life of the established theme. Consider a classroom where the educator has infused a camping theme throughout the space. Large-group instruction is centered around a tissue-paper campfire, the pointer stick becomes a marshmallow roasting stick, woodland creatures are found on the wall, stuffed animals ornament the shelves, forest soundtracks echo in the background, and tents are offered as a calming space. What messages do we deliver when we present a theme that does not consider learners' perspectives and overshadows their wonders, curiosities, and thinking? Because the learning environment itself serves as a teacher, its design must be intentional and responsive and offer multiple opportunities that move beyond a singular theme.

Theme-based concepts are sometimes developed and established before learners enter the space, so these themes emerge in tokenistic ways. For example, the preselected celebrations of the month often determine the life that the environment will breathe. During the month of February, in honor of Black History Month, tables are draped in kente cloth, bulletin boards are lined with the faces of children who represent the African diaspora, and the sign at the door greets learners in various African languages. While we do not believe that celebrating heritages is unimportant, we want to stress that these heritages live *beyond* a particular month and should be infused in meaningful ways throughout the year. We encourage you to collaborate with protagonists in researching the cultural appropriateness of what you offer within a space.

Missed Invitation 3: Spaces need to be heavily decorated.

Entering a space that is heavily decorated with a bombardment of colors, excessive patterns, too much furnishing, clutter, and disorganization negatively affects learners' abilities to process information. The space itself should not speak louder than the work and the voices of the children. Focusing on decoration highlights the aesthetics, which is not in service of learning but in favor of the educator's particular vision of beauty. A space designed with such an approach might cause learners to engage in hyperactive behavior, or it might induce an anesthetic-like reaction, resulting in a numbness, dulling, or diminishing of the senses.

We must not cloak ourselves in the comfort of clutter and sentiments. When you consider the environment to be a place of thinking and learning, you prioritize the invitations for learning that children interact with rather than the decor. Through co-creation of a space, we imagine an environment that highlights children's work—one where the visual and audio setting does not detract from but in fact amplifies the learning.

Missed Invitation 4: Spaces should be shifted immediately and frequently.

Making shifts in the environment is essential to the enrichment of learning; however, we must carefully consider why and how often we transform our spaces. It is important to remember that every change made to the environment tests a theory. Shifts should come with a plan—one that is responsive to observations made over time, through conversations, and in collaboration with protagonists to offer thoughtful designs. The changes we make to our environment require us to allow time for the theory to actualize itself. We also need to consider whether decisions are based on destructive mindsets that center the educator's assumptions and biases about learners. We must be responsive and intentional in the shifts we make and move beyond reactionary approaches made in haste.

Unraveling the Knots

Culturally responsive spaces encourage and invite dialogue, collaboration, ingenuity, and expression in honoring children's work. We must interrogate the traditional assumptions we hold when creating such spaces. Co-designing and establishing a community of learning is messy and requires a level of risk and exploration; it involves a journey through the unknown.

We must tease out the tensions, challenges, and wonderings to unveil the marvels of learning for ourselves and children. Join us in unraveling the knots we have discovered along this journey:

Knot 1: The outdoor learning environment is not used as a space for learning and is used only as a reward or for a break.

As educators, we have an obligation to provide intentional spaces, whether indoors or outdoors. The outdoor learning environment provides a plethora of opportunities for thinking and learning to occur. It must be viewed not only as a space for free play but also as a landscape for learning that is seamless. The intention of the environment shifts from space to space, driven by a plan that is co-initiated by the protagonists. Creating a sense of belonging to nature provides opportunities for inquiry that align with play-based approaches to learning. What messages are sent when the outdoor space is used in a static manner? How might the outdoor learning environment be used flexibly instead?

Knot 2: The educator has inherited a space that contradicts their own belief systems and presents challenges for revitalization.

You as the educator have visions for a space that speaks, and as you enter the learning environment, you encounter limits in achieving this goal. We understand this challenge. However, our offerings in the space have to be co-constructed with learners; the space must not assume the outdated or cluttered legacies that previously lived within it.

Consider repurposing the furnishings, materials, and layout of your space to maximize thinking and learning. We must reenvision and reinvigorate our spaces to allow for rich experiences to unfold (see chapter 3 for more discussion of this idea).

Knot 3: While safety should be a priority, it can be used in ways that hinder learners from taking risks, and it can serve as a form of control of the materials and space.

Safety in the learning environment is of the utmost priority, but we need to design spaces that allow learners to take the risks necessary for them to grow in their ability to problem-solve and innovate. Often the ways learners interact with materials help us better understand how they explore the world and come to new understandings. When we intervene too quickly and remove or control the use of materials, we deny learners the rights to co-ownership of the space. Some levels of risk offer opportunities for learners to build self-confidence and perseverance. We want our learners to be viewed and to see themselves as competent and capable beings as they live, learn, and grow.

Knot 4: Even if our classroom is a warm and welcoming space, the broader learning community can speak to exclusion.

When we design spaces of inclusion, we consider how they respond to learners within a broader learning context. Children who may not be well-connected to their own learning environments may seek refuge in a space that nurtures their sense of belonging and well-being. However, some school policies or traditional practices may prevent learners from moving freely within the larger learning community to meet their needs. We return to the notion of deservedness to examine how a space of beauty can easily become a place that is regulated as a border where the host educator serves to patrol and police which learners can enter. We aim to shift the narrative from a place of ownership that provides care only for the specific learners attached to a classroom to one that embraces the broader role of a caring adult. When educators assume this role, children in need might be welcomed into alternative environments that honor their Rights to Space before returning to their assigned learning communities. In thinking about your own learning environment, do the messages outside of your classroom walls also speak to these rights?

Knot 5: The aesthetics of a space can overpower the intention for learning.

Pretty pedagogy is an approach to designing a learning environment or learning opportunity. The focus is on the beauty, materials, and arrangement but lacks intention for learning and connection to children's Rights to Spaces. While we want to create spaces of beauty to welcome learners, we need to ensure that learning is cultivated to move beyond the aesthetics themselves.

Pursuing the Gift

As you pursue the gift of learning, we encourage you to take a closer look at your learning environment. You can consider taking these small shifts to allow your space to speak to all learners who inhabit it:

→ **Declutter your space.** Examine your learning environment carefully, and consider whether the resources, materials, and furniture contribute to learning. Remove old or outdated resources that are no longer functional, broken materials, or furniture pieces that are not effectively being used or are cluttering the space.

→ **Get organized.** Consider how you can display materials in a way that will spark more interest, foster independence, or capitalize on natural elements in the space (e.g., organizing pencils or crayons by color, organizing materials by shape or size, using neutral-colored containers or baskets to house materials, and making use of natural lighting).

→ **Map out where playful opportunities can be offered.** It is important to remember that not all learning needs to take place at a desk. As you consider shifting your space to being more flexible and fluid, view your physical space in this way; think about tops of shelving units that are accessible to learners, carpeted areas, window ledges, and more.

→ **Scan for accessibility and student input.** Consider removing items that are not accessible to learners or that have not been co-constructed (e.g., posters, photos that do not reflect the children in the space, materials on the walls that are placed very high and out of reach for learners).

Gifts of Learning

The learning environment is a space where living and learning co-exist. We invite you to think about how to design your space to respond to, challenge, and provide extensions for thinking. We now summarize the key concepts explored in this chapter:

→ The one hundred languages are tied to our memories and invite us to draw close to the many expressions of learning and thinking.

→ The environment itself is a teacher that relies on the protagonists (learners, families, educators, and community) and their contributions to the learning environment.

→ The learning environment is composed of four elements that seamlessly inhabit a space: time, physical space, materials, and relationships.

→ Designing spaces requires thoughtful planning that invites the one hundred languages and highlights connections to the curriculum in integrated ways.

→ Children have Rights to Spaces that illuminate their lived identities.

→ The flow of the day intentionally prepares learners to be successful within a learning space.

→ The learning environment must be flexible and repurposed to serve the learners who inhabit it.

As you seek the gifts we have offered you in this chapter, we encourage you to examine your learning environment to create a space that speaks. Reflect on these questions to reimagine your space:

→ Which of the one hundred languages speak loudly in the learning environment?

→ Which of the one hundred languages speak softly in the learning environment?

→ What shifts might you now consider?

→ Scan your entire space, and ask yourself what intentions live there. Why is the space arranged or organized in this way? Do the intentions center an adult perspective?

→ How might you shift or amend your intentions to honor all protagonists in the community?

→ How might the learning environment embody learners' Rights to Space?

→ How might you center thinking and learning?

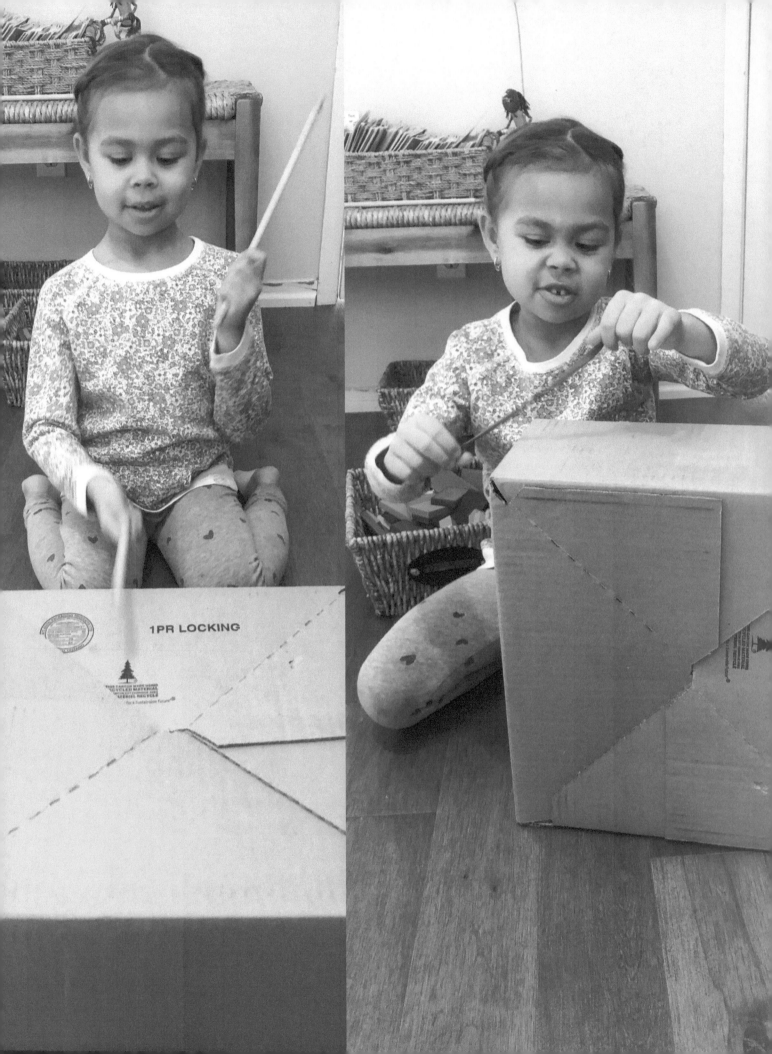

Chapter 3

Playful Pieces

After months of searching, you have selected the perfect gift to respond to the ongoing requests of a child in your life. This gift has been chosen with intention, wrapped with care, and offered with love. The day to present the gift has come, and you are anticipating the moment when the child will unwrap it. The celebration begins, and the moment arrives; the ribbon is undone, and the gift is revealed. The child marvels at what appears before them and is immediately drawn to the invitation to play. The child creates musical compositions, tells stories of magical dragons scaling a castle, shelters themselves from the ever-present danger of vampire bats, and creates armor that is worn with pride as they march off to their next adventure. The adults in the room marvel at the child's creativity and how mesmerized the child is by this present. In this moment, the true gift is revealed . . .

Can you recall an occasion when you received a gift as a child, and the gift wasn't the item that you were most enthralled with—instead, it was the wrapping paper, ribbon, or box that captured your interest most? Think about a moment from your childhood when you used the gifts offered by nature, such as stones, sticks, and other found materials, for countless hours of dramatic play and creative engagement.

Loose parts such as these are gifts that unleash a world of possibilities, joy, and learning. Children are inspired by these playful pieces that can easily transform play in a variety of ways.

The Theory of Loose Parts

In the 1970s, British architect Simon Nicholson coined the term *loose parts*. He maintained that creativity is not possessed only by a "gifted few"; instead, ingenuity is born from the curiosities of children as they interact with the world. Loose parts are open-ended materials that express a child's visions when manipulated, assembled, separated, stacked, and arranged (Nicholson 1972). With every touch of a playful piece, a child can unlock untold experiences. Through loose parts, children can direct their own learning, as these open-ended materials require no direction and provide multiple entry points for learners to make their thinking visible. A child's interests, strengths, and curiosities are revealed by the gift of these pieces as learners collaborate, communicate, cooperate, interact, and dialogue with one another in the process. Loose parts are essential tools that honor divergent and creative ways of thinking. No piece ever has to be used in the same way. Through play with loose parts, children are empowered by choice and have the autonomy to center their own theories, ideas, and learning.

Loose parts are relevant to every child. They cross the boundaries of gender, age, race, ability, socioeconomic status, religion, ethnicity, language, and more. They provide equitable opportunities for learners to express themselves, their experiences, and who they are. The use of loose parts opens various access points for learners to connect and relate to a variety of social identities. Different perspectives and interpretations are invited in play, and no one way is privileged over the other, as the use of loose parts promotes multiple learning outcomes and experiences.

Loose parts provide rich opportunities, as they not only support all the developmental domains (cognitive, social, physical, and emotional) but also support the curriculum in an integrated fashion. The open-ended nature of loose parts provokes possibilities.

The Great Debate: Toys versus Loose Parts

When play is prioritized in early years settings, programming often centers around the use of commercial toys, such as dollhouses, trains, farmhouses, and more. Often, the use of toys is deeply rooted in the inherited legacies of early years programming. As we consider what we gift to our learners, we must ask an essential question: Do the materials provide opportunities for learners to create their own theories, analyze multiple perspectives, and represent concepts? Toys are very specific in their function, often directing and providing formulaic outcomes that do not require higher-order thinking. Loose parts allow learners to develop ideas that tap into their personal experiences.

When we align our planning with Bloom's taxonomy, we consider the cognitive skills that learners engage in when playing with open-ended materials. Bloom's taxonomy provides a framework to support our understanding of the complexity of thinking that is possible as learners engage in play (see figure 3.1).

Figure 3.1. Making Connections to Toys and Loose Parts Using Bloom's Taxonomy

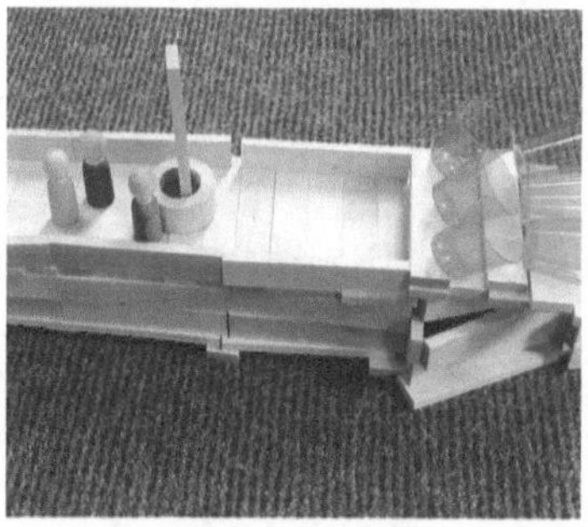

Toys		Loose Parts
Learners recall ideas that relate to the toy based on their prior knowledge.	**Remembering**	Learners recall ideas that relate to the object based on their prior knowledge.
The toy prescribes the type of play; learners can explain their play as it relates to what they know.	**Understanding**	The object created with loose parts emerges from learners' prior knowledge and understanding about the object.
Learners draw on their prior experiences, but the toy provides limited opportunities to problem solve beyond its function.	**Applying**	Learners apply their ideas in creating and designing their own objects.
Learners have limited options in testing their designs and reimagining their theories and ideas.	**Analyzing**	Learners reflect on their design process; they evaluate the design of their creation and make adjustments through problem solving and innovation.
Learners have limited opportunity to justify their choice of materials.	**Evaluating**	Learners justify the materials they have chosen to represent their thinking.
Learners have limited opportunity to assemble, design, and construct.	**Creating**	Learners formulate their own ideas about the object and create something using loose parts.

We invite you to consider the differences between offering children toys and offering them loose parts. When selecting materials, we should pose this question: "Who is doing the thinking, the toy or the child?" (Haughey 2017). Toys are specific in their function and dictate play experiences in predetermined ways. Consider the example illustrated in figure 3.1; when a child is given a toy boat, they may conjure memories, experiences, and knowledge connected to boats. This activation of the child's prior knowledge provides opportunities for them to access ideas about the boat, which then becomes the central focus for play. The boat might reveal stories of an excursion with a family member, retell a story of a popular television show, or reveal the child's inner imaginative stories of a boat that flies. The play assumes a common theme that dictates how the child interacts with the object and does not diverge far from it; thus, play has been outlined for the child.

Consider now the interaction learners might have with loose parts when given opportunities to engage with them over time. On the first day, they might create a boat, and on a subsequent day, they may reuse the materials to expand on their design, adding more details; on another day, they may use the loose parts to construct something completely different. Learners are not tied to one central theme; the loose parts provide multiple possibilities for engagement and interaction with the playful pieces. This process yields more opportunities for learners' thinking to become visible.

Sometimes, children want to broaden the boundaries of what a toy can do. However, because of the fixed nature of the toy, frustration arises when it does not align with their thoughts. For instance, we may hear learners protest, "I want it to turn into a robot, but it won't let me!" Conversely, we must consider whom certain toys are manufactured for, as well as what social identities they speak to. Children can be given a toy that they have little or no connection to, because the toy does not reflect their lived experiences. How often do we see dream dollhouses marketed to a specific gender? Rarely do we see more realistic representations of homes inhabited by diverse learners, such as co-ops and apartments. We must ask ourselves this question: Do learners truly connect to such toys, and what implicit messages do these toys send to a child?

We are not opposed to children using and engaging with toys in personal settings; however, in the learning environment, we must consider the use of loose parts and the instructional benefits they yield. To invite deep thinking, we encourage the use of these open-ended materials that allow learners to construct their own theories and bring them to life. Loose parts give learners the flexibility to evaluate, analyze, and make shifts and adaptations to their designs.

The Power to Manipulate

Historically, people around the world have interacted with physical objects to solve problems and make sense of abstract theories and concepts. Within the context of mathematics, effective practice has used manipulation as a means to deepen mathematical thinking. Manipulatives can support learners in transferring their mathematical skills by shifting from the concrete to the representational to the abstract. "The theory of experiential education revolves around the idea that learning is enhanced when students acquire knowledge through active processes that engage them" (Hartshorn and Boren 1990, as cited in Hand2Mind, n.d., para. 4). We challenge educators to think about how we might offer materials for learners to manipulate similarly in *all* subject areas. We are not suggesting a debate of whether a math manipulative can serve as a loose part; we are stressing the importance and power of manipulation to support, scaffold, and facilitate learners' understanding of concepts.

When we offer playful pieces that learners can manipulate seamlessly within our programs, we enable these opportunities:

→ Children can make their thinking visible.

→ Learners can express their abstract ideas in concrete ways.

→ Children can take ownership of their learning.

→ A diverse range of learners with various needs can confidently engage in problem solving, testing, and analyzing their ideas.

→ Educators can motivate and capture learners' interests while accessing multiple areas of the curriculum.

With all the benefits that manipulation has to offer, we question why it is not centered beyond the realm of mathematics. When offering visual art experiences, educators would never deprive learners of artistic tools and materials. Since research validates the importance of manipulation, we should transfer this approach to all areas of curriculum. Loose parts can serve as the tools that facilitate play and thinking for children in all learning contexts.

Leveraging Loose Parts

Loose parts are the medium used to express children's visions and desires. They honor divergent thinking and allow us to speak to the varied needs and learning styles of the children who inhabit our learning spaces. We must consider whether the materials that we offer provide fixed or flexible play experiences (see figure 3.2).

Figure 3.2. Play Experiences for Fixed and Open-Ended Materials

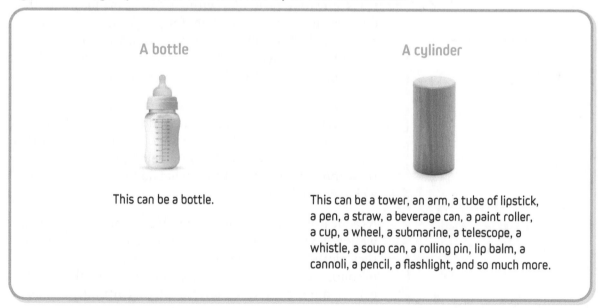

A bottle

This can be a bottle.

A cylinder

This can be a tower, an arm, a tube of lipstick, a pen, a straw, a beverage can, a paint roller, a cup, a wheel, a submarine, a telescope, a whistle, a soup can, a rolling pin, lip balm, a cannoli, a pencil, a flashlight, and so much more.

The power of playful pieces is unleashed when learners have the autonomy to manipulate open-ended materials in ways that promote their cultural beliefs. Sharing values through loose parts provides space for divergent thought to be centered and affirmed. This process supports and enhances the development of creative and critical-thinking skills. When children have opportunities to see various modes of thought, we provide them with a blueprint for understanding that people think differently in the world.

> When children develop critical and divergent thinking and can generate ideas about differences and similarities, they gain appreciation for diversity and can engage in social justice work. In other words, the more children play with loose parts, the more they may develop the thinking skills that will help them understand differences and similarities and engage in the process of positive societal change. (Daly and Beloglovsky 2018, 9)

Loose parts are equitable materials because they appeal to a wide range of children who hold various social identities. Loose parts transcend the classifications of class, race, religion, ability, socioeconomic status, gender, ethnicity, age, language, and sexual orientation. Loose parts are tools of liberation because learners are not bound by the social constructs underlying commercial toy manufacturing and marketing. Loose parts provide uninhibited opportunities for children to express themselves creatively, critically, and in socially conscious ways. The very definition of their use is determined by the child who reveals the inner life of a playful piece. Through this interaction, learners' lived experiences emerge.

> Because loose parts are open-ended and are free of biases and stereotypes, all children can interact with them equally, without any preloaded ideas of how they ought to be used. (Daly and Beloglovsky 2018, 8)

When learners are offered fixed materials in the learning environment, we often see power dynamics that reflect the societal injustices of the larger world. We may observe learners playing with a predetermined object in ways that affirm stereotypes and become gendered. For example, learners might say, "The cooking area is only for girls to play with," or "You can't play with this doll because its skin is too light for you. That baby couldn't be yours." At times, children perpetuate a sense of ownership and entitlement when they interact with toys and only invite particular learners into their play experiences.

We have also observed occasions when children use a toy in unconventional ways, and other children manage the play or dictate how the toy should be used. We question how this impacts learners and their sense of belonging. If we allow these interactions to continue, what do they mean for the well-being of learners?

As educators, we must also be mindful of the power dynamics we assert when we observe and respond to such oppressive rhetoric. When children display these dynamics in relation to commercialized toys, they may replicate inequities that exist in our society. If we have adopted a culturally responsive

Playful Note

When introducing loose parts, gather learners in a circle and present a loose part to them. Pass the item around the circle, and invite learners to imagine the possibilities. You may generate thinking by asking, "What could this be?" Be sure to document the ideas shared.

approach to teaching, then it is important that we act upon these injustices. By offering children open-ended materials, we provide multiple entry points for learners to express themselves in ways that are unhindered by the fixed nature of the materials. We invite you to consider the thought processes that learners engage with when offered fixed and open-ended materials (see figure 3.3).

Figure 3.3. Thought Processes of a Child Offered Fixed and Open-Ended Materials

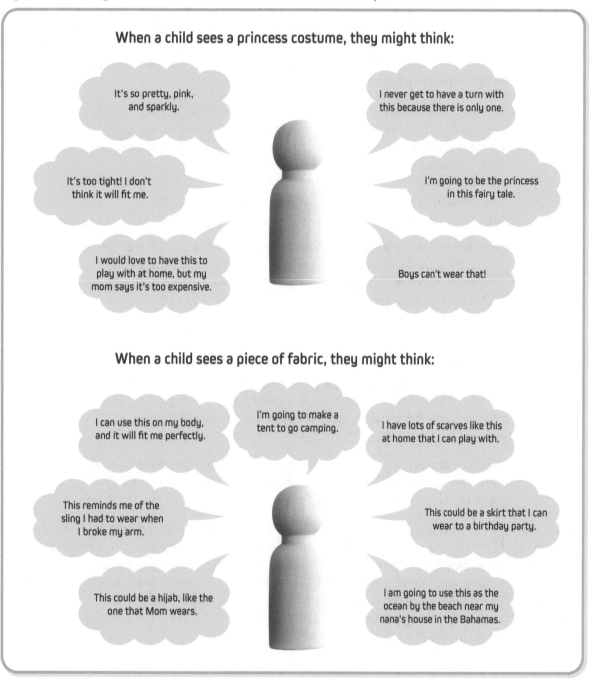

Loose Parts and Culturally Relevant Pedagogy

Children's worldviews are shaped and influenced by their interactions with playful pieces. "Play is the vehicle for learning" (Ontario Ministry of Education 2016b), and loose parts are the engine that drives learners to express themselves freely. The undefined nature of these playful pieces gives learners the freedom to challenge and critique societal norms. Through intentional offerings, educators can leverage loose parts as an entry point to have discussions with learners in critically conscious ways. Learners' contributions cannot be stifled, because these pieces highlight and honor their core beliefs in a way where they feel empowered. Barriers are broken when children enact their visions for social change through manipulation of playful parts, as shown in this classroom experience:

> As virtual teachers, we invited our learners to respond to the silent short film Ian (produced by Mundoloco CGI Ian Foundation). This film is about a boy who uses a wheelchair and expresses his desire to play on the playground with other children but is unable to because it is inaccessible. We asked learners how they might help Ian. Through the use of loose parts at home, children designed a variety of structures, devices, and mechanisms that would help Ian.

> Some learners built playgrounds with ramps, while others built elevator lifts and wider tunnels for him to maneuver through. Other learners used their loose parts to demonstrate different ways they could play with Ian without the use of a playground structure.

> As educators, we facilitated conversations around accessibility, and learners began to make connections to their own lived experiences. One learner expressed that the playground near their home would not be accessible for Ian and questioned how this could be changed. Other learners expressed frustration with elevators in their high-rise apartment buildings being out of service, and they wondered what it might mean for Ian if he lived in a building like theirs.

> Learners' desires to make spaces more accessible allowed us to engage in rich discussions around access and how they could make a difference and create social change in their own communities.

The use of open-ended materials shifts and changes as learners' lived experiences reveal the dynamics of culture. Space is provided for children to represent their theories, curiosities, and truth. The pieces amplify and assert learners' thoughts. When loose parts connect to learners' cultural identities (e.g., ikat fabric or bangles), children form even deeper connections to the materials. They have the power and autonomy to choose how they will interact with each playful piece, and they bring purpose to their creations. Loose parts provide a platform for families to access memories and share oral histories, traditions, and generational stories.

Playful pieces foster equitable outcomes that differentiate learners' needs, strengths, and curiosities while supporting the curriculum and assessment in an integrated manner. Through loose parts, teaching and learning are transformative and nurture high-yield strategies.

The Seven Types of Loose Parts

Educators sometimes assume that loose parts are only small, shiny, non-plastic, and expensive materials. However, Haughey (2017) organizes loose parts into seven types.

Fabric and ribbon

Wood reuse

Nature-based

Packaging

Metal

Plastic

Ceramic and glass

Playful Note

Invite learners to collect their own loose parts at home and bring them to the learning environment to support your programming.

These categories provide insight into the diverse range of materials that can be welcomed into our spaces. When we offer a variety of open-ended materials over time, learners' engagement increases, and their play becomes more purposeful in nature. After children have made connections to existing loose parts in the environment, new playful pieces can be offered to rejuvenate play.

Through our understanding of the seven types of loose parts, we can tap into a variety of materials that are economically sound and diverse. Playful pieces are accessible and can be found practically everywhere. Consider taking a walk and collecting the gifts nature has to offer; thrift stores, recycling centers, dollar stores, businesses that discard materials, garage sales, and even your own home can serve as great sources for finding loose parts as well. We expand our repertoire when we think beyond the way items are marketed or purposed.

The beauty of these materials stems from their ability to speak to learners' cultural competencies. Incorporating items that are culturally relevant, such as cowrie shells, batik fabric, or dried bamboo sticks, will present opportunities for children to make meaningful connections to the materials. Representation matters in our spaces, so we must consider this when we are intentionally selecting loose parts to use for the learning opportunities we are planning.

The Language of Schema

> It is exploration time, and as children scatter to the Invitations for Learning that intrigue them, Mimi searches the space, wandering from one opportunity to another and dragging her hands across the various materials. Her eyes are immediately drawn to a basket holding a collection of new shimmering loose parts. She races over to unearth the basket's contents, letting out a joyful squeal as she dumps the playful pieces onto the ground. The clatter of the materials drives her to grab handfuls and repetitively sprinkle them over the loose parts on the floor.
>
> Mimi then indulges in her delight by carefully selecting a few pieces and arranging them to erect her creation. She pounds her fist against the arrangement as the loose parts scatter and the creation becomes undone. Mimi repeats this process two more times, attempting to build her creation higher each time.

In this moment shared with Mimi, so much learning has been revealed to the observer and to the child. A moment like this captures the interwoven threads of thought evoked by the interaction with materials.

When listening to and observing children with intention, we are invited to see this experience as a learning opportunity—one that imparts the wisdom of the child and how they explore their world. Jean Piaget characterizes schemas as repetitive patterns of thought or behaviors that organize information (Stacey 2019). We can make sense of play through the ongoing behaviors exhibited by a child, which present their inner desires and interests.

Schemas are a form of symbolic language that a child uses to communicate through their play with loose parts. When observing children during play, we may notice that they exhibit behaviors that align with one dominant schema or many schemas at the same time. Once the educator interprets the repetitive behaviors, threads of thought are illuminated, and these can then be used to design appropriate learning opportunities. Using loose parts develops and nurtures the mental framework of schemas at play. Schemas act as a means to discover and explore the curiosities that create brain pathways for foundational learning. Figure 3.4 shows examples of loose parts connected to some of the schematic behaviors as suggested by Michelle Thornhill (2015).

Figure 3.4. The Connection of Loose Parts to Schematic Behaviors

Schema	Connecting	Disconnecting and Deconstructing	Enclosing and Enveloping	Transforming
Materials	 Paper clips Popsicle sticks Corks Velcro strips	 Tissue paper Pine cones Yarn Dominoes	 Plastic cups Ribbon Scarves Twine	 Peg people Feathers Bead necklaces Wire

Schema	Ordering and Positioning	Transporting	Dynamic Horizontal	Dynamic Vertical
Materials	 Wood chips Wood cubes Candles Bingo chips	 Buttons Measuring cup Plastic caps Felt balls	 Rocks Wood beads Wood logs Straws Metal springs	 Wood rings Elastic bands Marbles Clothespins Wood blocks

Through intentional, purposeful planning and communication with families and caregivers, we can select materials to support learners and move them forward in their play and thinking. We can then adjust our pedagogical approaches and what we offer to include concepts that meet the standards of the curriculum. Piaget purports that a schema is "a thread of thought that is demonstrated by repeated patterns in children's play, meaning that children's play is a reflection of deeper internally and specifically directed thoughts. When children are exploring schemas, they are building understandings of abstract ideas, patterns, and concepts" (Curtis and Jaboneta 2019, 7).

Read Mimi's story on page 80 again. Then we invite you to consider these questions as they relate to her story:

→ What repeated behaviors does Mimi exhibit?

→ What loose parts could you provide to build Mimi's schema in play?

→ How might our assumptions and beliefs have interfered in this interpretation of learning?

Through play, Mimi explores the materials using her senses. She finds comfort in the sounds that she creates as she sprinkles materials. We see that Mimi is building vertically, which indicates to the educator that she is displaying the dynamic vertical schema. Her desire to pound her fists against the materials resulted in them scattering to the floor; this behavior is connected to the deconstructing schema. As we think about what loose parts to offer to Mimi, it is important to consider offering sensory experiences that connect to the schemas she has displayed. The educator may consider offering Mimi cardboard pieces, plastic ice cubes, and dominoes, as these loose parts might support her need to deconstruct her creations while creating safer conditions for play. Mimi might also benefit from spools, stacking rocks, or empty boxes to enhance her vertical creations and to support problem solving and innovation. To encourage Mimi to build with more purpose, the educator might offer photographs of structures found in her community or the world as inspiration. Initially, one might view Mimi's behavior and use of the materials as destructive. However, if we hold such biases we may fail to consider Mimi's desire to explore the properties of the materials (e.g., the sounds they make when they scatter), the ways in which the materials are impacted by change, and the elements of cause and effect, all of which are deeply rooted in scientific exploration. We encourage educators to observe the behaviors exhibited during play carefully, as this drives the materials and experiences we offer to children.

Creating Conditions for Play with Loose Parts

Learning with loose parts requires ongoing dialogue with children. We must co-construct with learners the *how*: how to care for, handle, and use open-ended materials to yield optimal learning in play. An entry point might be co-constructing expectations and how the materials will be used in the learning environment. It is important to ensure that these principles are approached through a positive lens and are reflective of our beliefs about learners. Consider the language that is used and its accessibility to learners and families. We offer an example on the next page.

Our Playful Promise

Our loose parts are treasures that we need to treat with care.

As we use them, we will show respect and always try to share.

We can use them for our thinking, to show what we know.

Every day we use them, they will help us learn and grow.

When we are done, we promise we will put them all away,

So that we have them for our learning and to use another day.

Scaffolding Loose Parts

To deepen learners' interactions with loose parts, we should provide guided learning experiences in which the playful pieces are used more intentionally. We need to slow down the process so that learners tap into a metacognitive state, helping children to think about their own thinking. Our approaches should be intentional and grounded in our observations of learners and their connections with the materials.

The scaffolding of learning conditions must be layered with multiple experiences for children to be guided in the meaningful use of loose parts. Observations and documentation are essential to planning and scaffolding learning in the early stages.

Our observations can facilitate our thinking and planning around how to envision the loose parts in new ways that connect to the curriculum. Through large-group, small-group, and individual experiences, a child like Mimi can be provoked to reimagine playful pieces in a comprehensive fashion. Loose parts serve as a conduit to a child's new thinking and affirm their understanding.

The following protocol can support learners in the use of open-ended materials:

1. Observe
2. Think
3. Explore
4. Create
5. Communicate and document

This next section illustrates this protocol through an example from our own classroom experience.

Creating Intentional Experiences with Loose Parts

We may introduce loose parts to learners by inspiring them with a concrete image or video to replicate. This is an accessible way to begin engaging learners with playful pieces.

As you prepare this type of experience, you should intentionally select playful pieces that set learners up for success, taking these considerations into account:

→ **Types of loose parts**: Ensure that the loose parts will support learners in achieving the desired effect of the photo or video. For example, you can offer popsicle sticks that might be used for plant stems.

- → **Color palette:** Think about the color scheme observed in the photo or video. Select materials that reflect these shades and colors.

- → **Quantity:** Remember that less is more. Providing smaller amounts gives children the opportunity to think carefully, problem-solve, and be innovative in using the materials.

- → **Organization:** Ensure that materials are organized and accessible for small groups of learners. Placing materials in small trays, bowls, cutlery organizers, and so on enables learners to observe the materials and access them easily.

- → **Parameters:** Choose a background surface on which learners will work and display their creations. You can use a tile, a picture frame, a wood slice, a piece of construction paper, or a mat.

In our own classroom experience, we have shared the following photo of a hibiscus flower with learners and invited them to create their interpretations with loose parts. Figure 3.5 illustrates how we organized the loose parts and presented them to learners, along with the considerations we made when planning this learning experience.

Figure 3.5. Organization and Presentation of Loose Parts and Considerations Made When Planning This Learning Experience

Types of loose parts: The educator has offered a variety of materials that span the seven types of loose parts (wood beads, buttons, pipe cleaners, plastic pieces, and candles).

Color palette: The colors of the loose parts are those seen in the hibiscus flower (red, green, and yellow).

Quantity: Small numbers of materials are offered to learners.

Organization: Materials are organized by color and shape in a divided tray.

Parameters: The educator provides a wood picture frame to support learners in recognizing a work space to share their creations.

Before engaging learners in this experience, we reviewed our co-constructed learning expectations (presented earlier as "Our Playful Promise"). The table on the following page provides a guide for this activity, based on how we navigated this experience with learners by working through each step of the protocol for using open-ended materials.

Protocol Steps	Teacher Actions	Learner Actions

Observe

→ Invite learners to observe the materials with their hands on their laps.

→ Prompt learners with these questions:

What do you see?

What do you notice?

→ If learners need further prompting, ask:

What colors do you see?

What shapes do you see?

→ Record responses shared by learners.

→ Learners observe the properties of the materials.

→ They share their observations, based on the teacher's prompts (e.g., "I see the color red," "There are gems; some are soft, and others are hard").

Think

→ Invite learners to think about what they will do with the materials.

→ Prompt learners with this question:

What can you do with the materials you see?

→ Record responses shared by learners.

→ Learners continue to observe the materials with their hands in their laps.

→ They share ways they might use the materials (e.g., "I can create a tower with the cubes").

Explore

→ Invite learners to explore the materials by using their senses. Ask them to touch the materials, manipulate the materials, listen to the sounds the materials make, or make other observations.

→ Prompt learners by asking:

What do you now notice?

→ Record responses shared by learners.

→ Learners touch and manipulate the materials.

→ Learners may also test materials to explore their properties (e.g., by dropping items on the floor).

→ Learners share additional ideas connected to their observations and exploration.

Protocol Steps	Teacher Actions	Learner Actions
Create 	→ Share a photo of the hibiscus flower and ask: *How can you represent the hibiscus flower?* → Provide learners with a parameter (e.g., wood slice, piece of construction paper, tile) to use in constructing their creations. → Observe and document what learners say, do, and represent.	→ Learners review the photo and use it as a source of inspiration for their creations. → Learners construct their creations with the materials and parameter.
Communicate and Document 	→ Ask learners to engage in a "gallery move," where they move around the room to see the various representations made by other learners.* → Ask learners to communicate their wonderings and questions about each creation: *What does this make you think about?* → Provide opportunities for learners to capture their thinking (e.g., by taking a photo, by drawing a picture, by sharing thoughts orally, or by writing). → Use shared writing experiences to represent learners' thinking.	→ Learners move carefully within the space to observe how materials have been used by their peers. → Learners celebrate their peers' creations. → They share their thoughts and wonderings connected to the experience. → They document their thinking through drawings, words, photography, and so on.

*The term *gallery move* disrupts notions or concepts about ability, bodies, and movement. The use of the term *gallery walk* excludes learners who access movement in a variety of ways. We challenge you to reflect on the words you use in your classroom and how they may affect learners.

Comprehensive Loose Parts Programming

A comprehensive loose parts program provides opportunities within the flow of the day for learners to engage in whole-group, small-group, and independent learning experiences (see figure 3.6). When organizing your comprehensive loose parts program, you need to ensure that it aligns with a gradual release of responsibility model, much like a comprehensive literacy program. It should include these types of experiences:

→ **Modeled:** Through modeled learning experiences, we adopt an "I do; you watch" approach, where the educator models and shares how learners might use the loose parts with purpose. As the educator manipulates the open-ended materials, they use a think-aloud strategy to articulate the actions they are undertaking. Through their demonstrations, the educator may ask questions that children answer as they engage with the loose parts.

→ **Shared:** Shared learning experiences provide opportunities for children to be invited into the co-construction and manipulation of loose parts to represent their thoughts and ideas around a central task or learning goal. This is an "I do; you help" approach. Shared experiences can take place in both whole-group and small-group instruction. The educator may use a text, an image, or a question to provoke learners to use the materials and respond, represent, or reimagine how loose parts are used and can be used together. Documentation can reveal to the educator the ways learners are using materials.

→ **Guided:** In guided opportunities with loose parts, the educator and children are working together to create more intention in play. This is a "we do together" approach. The educator may scaffold experiences they have modeled and shared with a small group of learners who require more scaffolding. They invite learners to engage with loose parts as they guide them with questions and support. The educator may pair learners who use open-ended materials in creative ways with learners who require more opportunities to deepen their learning.

→ **Independent:** In independent play, learners are invited to innovate and create with loose parts that are intentionally placed in the learning environment. The children engage with playful pieces with purpose based on the thinking they have gained through modeled, shared, and guided learning opportunities. They now are independently attending to loose parts in ways that demonstrate the learning acquired from the gradual release model. The educator continues to document how learners interact with materials, and uses what is gathered to support next steps for planning and programming future modeled, shared, and guided experiences.

Playful Note

Scaffolding the use of loose parts can be done individually or in small groups, depending on learners' needs.

Figure 3.6. Gradual Release of Responsibility Using Loose Parts

Level of Educator Support			
High	Whole-group instruction	Modeled I do. You watch.	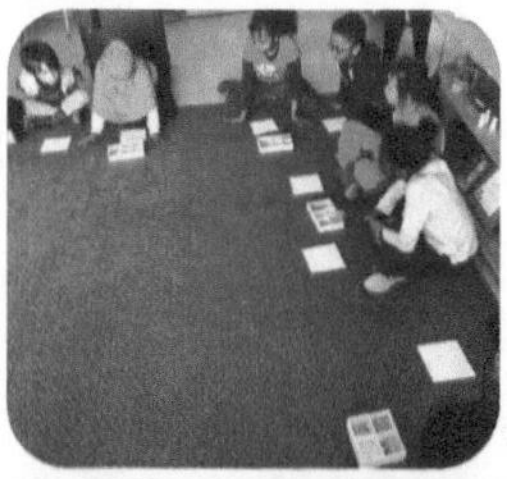
	Whole-group or small-group instruction	Shared I do. You help.	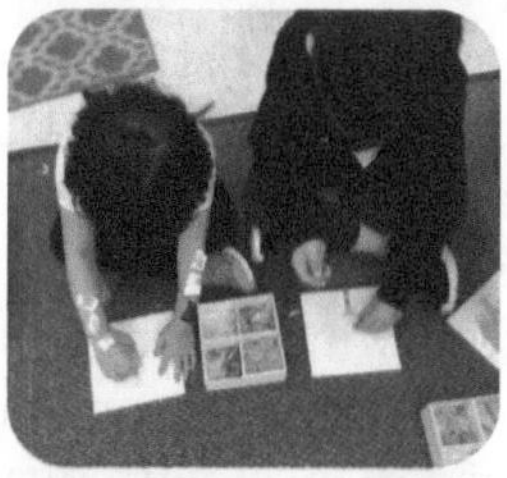
	Small-group instruction	Guided We do together.	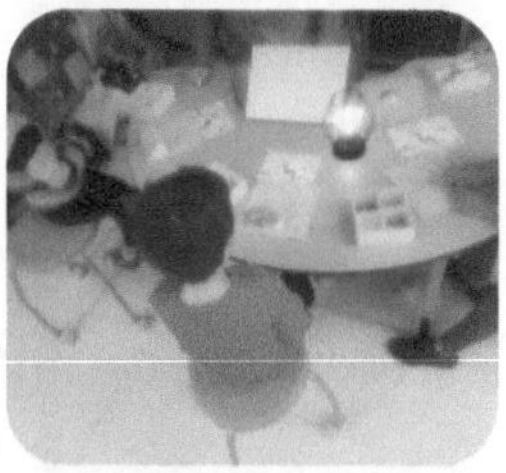
Low	Loose parts in play	Independent You do. I watch.	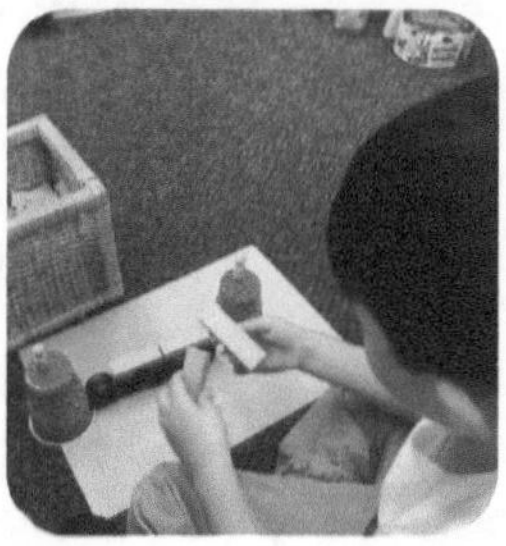

Strategic Actions for Loose Parts

As you engage in a comprehensive loose parts program, we encourage you to consider the following strategic actions defined by Pat Johnson:

Modeling: Clearly demonstrating what you want the learner to do, using explicit language

Scaffolding: Supporting the learner; doing it with them

Prompting: Saying something that will remind the child to try the strategy or behavior

Backing Off: Letting your supports fade away, dismantling your scaffolds so that the child takes more responsibility for initiating the strategy or behavior

Reinforcing: Naming the strategy or behavior that the child used, praising it, and showing them how it worked in this instance (Johnson 2006, 8–9)

Engaging with Loose Parts

In play, we observe various forms of engagement with loose parts. Learners may represent their thinking through abstract representation, exploration, construction, or replication (see figures 3.7 and 3.8). As a provocateur, we extract meaning from the information gathered in documentation to go deeper in learning and programming. When we consider what was revealed about Mimi in play, it becomes clear that she was engaged in the phase of exploration. Presenting opportunities for Mimi to replicate in whole-group and small-group settings may enrich her experiences with playful pieces in relation to curriculum.

Figure 3.7. Engagement with Loose Parts

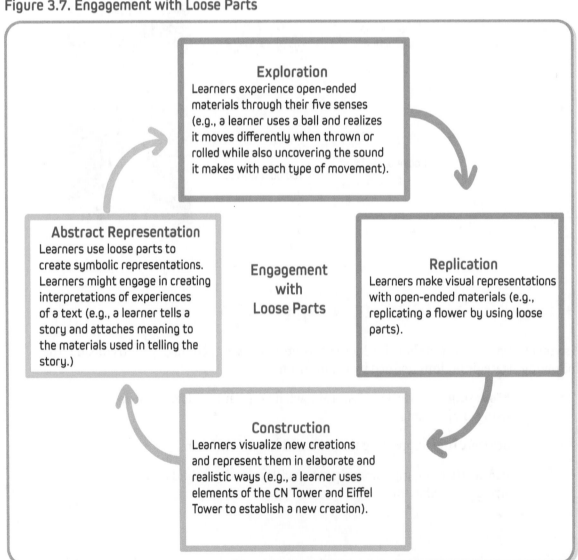

Exploration
Learners experience open-ended materials through their five senses (e.g., a learner uses a ball and realizes it moves differently when thrown or rolled while also uncovering the sound it makes with each type of movement).

Abstract Representation
Learners use loose parts to create symbolic representations. Learners might engage in creating interpretations of experiences of a text (e.g., a learner tells a story and attaches meaning to the materials used in telling the story.)

Engagement with Loose Parts

Replication
Learners make visual representations with open-ended materials (e.g., replicating a flower by using loose parts).

Construction
Learners visualize new creations and represent them in elaborate and realistic ways (e.g., a learner uses elements of the CN Tower and Eiffel Tower to establish a new creation).

Figure 3.8. Representations of Engagement with Loose Parts

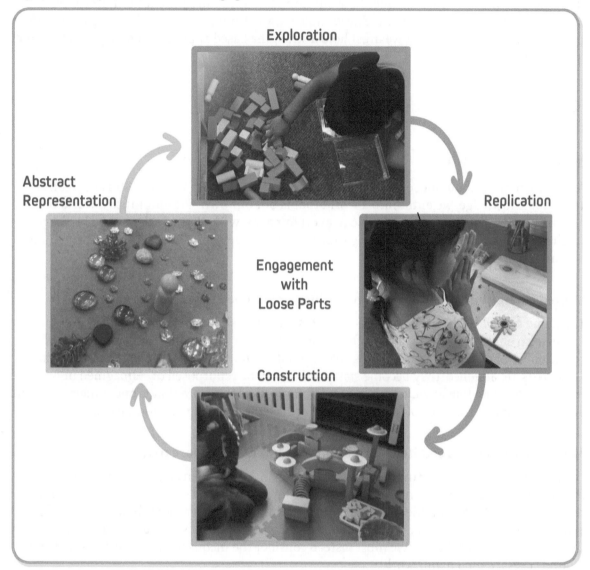

Safety in the Learning Environment

As educators, we are continuously working to ensure that we are promoting safe conditions for ourselves and our learners. We must be attentive and responsive to learners in ways that prioritize health and safety. As you gift playful pieces to children, it is important to remember that the guidelines we offer here are only suggestions. We encourage you to follow the safety guidelines of your school district.

To promote safety, it is essential to understand learners and their developmental needs and diverse interests. For younger learners who may be tempted to place materials in their mouths, consider presenting larger playful items that limit the possibility for ingestion. You can use small-object choking testers to determine whether the loose parts are safe for play. Adopt cleaning and sanitizing protocols to ensure that materials are washed and sterilized on a regular basis.

Remember to always reflect on the schemas. How are learners navigating the materials? As facilitators of play, we must consider how our implicit biases can influence our decisions in controlling the use of loose parts. We need to steer away from policing under the guise of safety. To create conditions for safety, we must hold a strengths-based approach, remain reflective, and center learners' voices.

Additional Considerations

Missed Invitations

As we learn more about loose parts as precious gifts that unwrap learners' stories, creativity, and prior knowledge, we enter into a world that is not our own. We enter into a world of play filled with potential. If we choose to avert our eyes, we lose the insights and brilliance small moments have to offer us. Along the way, misconceptions can arise about the use and potential of loose parts:

Missed Invitation 1: Loose parts can be glued or fastened to create a product.

The name *loose parts* should be honored—that is, the parts should remain loose. We seek to create an environment that allows these pieces to be moved, manipulated, and arranged continuously. Spaces that speak to loose parts should not provide materials that fasten. When loose parts are attached, they become static and cannot be repurposed or reimagined in new ways. The parts no longer yield learning and become fixed in a state that is one-dimensional and product-driven. In this type of scenario, we do not see the thinking of children evolve over time.

Missed Invitation 2: Food items can be offered and used as loose parts.

Loose parts bring a diverse range of possibilities, flexibility, and sensory allure into a space; they provide children with multiple entry points for learning and expression. It is important to remember that the playful pieces we offer speak volumes to our learners about what is valued and honored. Inviting learners to playfully interact with food sends subconscious messages that food can be played with. We must instead consider the inequities and injustices that exist around access to food in our world.

Missed Invitation 3: Loose parts appeal only to the earliest of learners.

Loose parts transcend all grade levels. At any age, these playful pieces serve as pedagogical tools that integrate curriculum and leverage learning in rich ways. The potential of loose parts lives within the pieces, and the individual learner's interaction reveals the variables. Loose parts should live in learning spaces that extend beyond the early years, as they can serve as a mode of communication for any individual. Play is a right for *all* children and moves beyond the borders of early learning.

Missed Invitation 4: Loose parts can be offered in an isolated area within the learning environment.

Loose parts should never live in isolation. The parts are meant to be flexible, loose, and transported to other areas within the learning space, and they add value to other materials.

We know that many educators want to begin their journey with an area dedicated to loose parts, but we caution you to consider what values are in play when we do not honor loose parts throughout the learning environment. If we offer an isolated space for loose parts, power dynamics emerge that may lead to chaos and disruption of learning, and the potential that could have been unleashed in that space is stifled.

Missed Invitation 5: Once I have established expectations for loose parts, I do not have to revisit them.

Setting conditions is ongoing; it is not something done once and then abandoned. The conditions for learning and thinking take time to be established and require opportunities for revisiting and reenvisioning with learners throughout the year.

Unraveling the Knots

Loose parts foster creativity, innovation, communication, and collaboration. As we create spaces using loose parts to liberate learners' voices, we invite promise—a promise to reenvision play in the early years and abandon the methods we once considered progressive. As we open the gift of learning, we also need to undo the knots and tensions that restrain our ability to see the gift.

Knot 1: Educators impose their beliefs about and interpretations of loose parts on learners, which silences their stories and ideas.

We want to ensure that learners' theories are validated. As provocateurs, we want to ignite the thinking that is waiting to be released through the use of loose parts. In aiming for this, we need to remember that learners need to take the lead in sharing their own stories and ideas. When educators impose their thinking on learners' creativity, it is no longer the work of the child; it becomes the work of the educator. Play involves freedom for learners; once adults interject their own theories, perspectives, and biases, they introduce power dynamics and tensions in play and replicate oppressive structures.

For example, an educator observes learners moving wood cylinders in pathways around the carpet and exclaims, "Oh, wow! Look at the trains that are moving." A child responds, "It's not a train; it's my sea monster!" The educator replies, "But it can definitely be a train. Tomorrow we can build a train station here with signs and tracks, and we can go on an adventure."

Knot 2: The children will be sad and not want to play with loose parts if I take away their favorite toys.

As educators, we have the best of intentions for our learners. And although we intend to draw on learners' interests, our impact may cloud the authenticity of what they are truly invested in doing through play.

For instance, an educator feels like they cannot get rid of a dollhouse because the learners love it so much. The educator should consider the stories and theories that can emerge through loose parts, as opposed to what can be produced through playing with the dollhouse. We do not deny that children love toys, as they should, but we must provide opportunities for their thinking to emerge. We need to navigate and balance play in a way that honors the curriculum.

Knot 3: Math manipulatives can be used as loose parts.

We must remember that math manipulatives are designed to support mathematical concepts and thinking. Research shows that math manipulatives invite learners to engage in math processes through cognitive models and assist learners in communicating with their educators about these processes. Loose parts serve a similar intention, where children construct their own cognitive theories through abstract concepts, which play out through the materials they use. Although many things can be defined as loose parts, math manipulatives have a specific intended purpose.

An environment that houses a rich collection of loose parts will support learners and provide the canvas on which mathematical thinking and processes are demonstrated. When math manipulatives are not used for their intended purpose, we must reflect and question what messages are being sent to learners.

Knot 4: Scaffolding is required to teach children how to play.

The beauty of playful pieces is that no instructions are required. Play is a never-ending process and materials can be used in countless ways. Scaffolding experiences are instead meant to tap into learners' abilities to utilize the materials. We invite you to consider the loose parts protocol in a way that supports loose parts play and does not stifle the integrity of play.

Pursuing the Gift

Pursuing the gift of learning requires small steps that are accessible and achievable for play with loose parts. Here are some recommendations to inspire your practice:

→ **Start a collection of loose parts.** Ask families or other educators to contribute open-ended materials that can be used for play. Gather recyclables, explore thrift stores and local dollar stores, or consider what items you might be able to find in nature.

→ **"Rock what you got."** Consider what open-ended materials you already have in your classroom that could be used in your loose parts program. For example, look carefully at the open-ended materials you already own, such as cubes or bingo chips. Or gather items that support your art program, such as pom-poms, popsicle sticks, and pipe cleaners. These playful pieces can be used initially while you work to transition more open-ended materials into your everyday practice.

→ **Get organized.** Gather and collect a variety of containers that are neutral in tone (e.g., cutlery organizers, trays, egg cartons, desk caddies). Remember also that learners do not need copious amounts of materials; in fact, smaller amounts will invite more intentional use of loose parts, so your containers do not need to be very large.

→ **Invite learners to explore.** Co-construct the loose parts pledge, and use it with a simple scaffolding experience so that learners begin to get familiar with the materials. Using simple photographs serves as a great entry point for engagement.

Gifts of Learning

The gifts of learning exist within playful pieces. We have explored the learning possibilities that emerge when children represent their ideas and theories through loose parts. To summarize the key concepts explored in this chapter:

→ The theory of loose parts informs and supports learning and programming.

→ Loose parts differ from commercialized toys; they have specific benefits toys cannot offer.

→ Manipulation benefits thinking across all disciplines, not just math.

→ Open-ended materials provide windows into learners' thinking as they develop through play.

→ Loose parts can support culturally relevant pedagogy as it relates to social identities.

→ Loose parts can be categorized into seven types that support schemas through play.

→ We can create conditions that enhance the use of loose parts through a gradual release approach.

As you review these key takeaways from the chapter, we encourage you to envision a comprehensive loose parts program for your learning environment. Reflect on these questions to determine your next steps:

→ What playful pieces can you offer that connect to learners' interests, experiences, and identities?

→ How can the loose parts schemas support you in better understanding learners?

→ How can you affirm learners' cultural identities through loose parts play?

→ What whole-group and small-group scaffolding opportunities can you implement to support the conditions for learning?

Chapter 4
Inviting Learning

A treasured memory is the lasting gift of time well spent.

—*Tim Fargo*

The power of a loose part stems from the memories that it holds. A loose part is timeless and limitless, and it has the potential to communicate untold stories. Take a look at the loose parts pictured at the left.

- Which type of playful piece resonates with you the most?

- How might this loose part connect to a joyful memory in your childhood?

- What feelings does this item evoke for you?

The learning experiences we offer in our spaces have the potential to conjure memories, evoke feelings, and provoke thinking. They require planning, intention, and creativity. When we invite learning, we offer pleasurable moments that inspire children and create everlasting memories for them.

What Is an Invitation for Learning?

An Invitation for Learning is a beautiful arrangement of playful pieces that are intentionally chosen to provoke children's curiosity as they make connections and discoveries to enhance their understanding of the world. We think of these as gifts that children unwrap to unleash the possibilities of thinking and learning through play, exploration, and investigation.

The Invitation for Learning in figure 4.1 includes the wordless text *Another* by Christian Robinson and features colorful transparent blocks, plastic ice cubes, bead necklaces, plastic rods, and transparent geometric pieces, along with wood peg people, small disco balls, and dry-erase markers placed on the surface of a light panel.

Figure 4.1. Sample Invitation for Learning: *Another* by Christian Robinson

The Invitation for Learning in figure 4.2 presents *Where Are You From?* by Yamile Saied Mendez, a book about a girl who journeys with her grandfather to learn about her cultural heritage. The invitation also offers blocks with arrows, rocks, sea glass, beads, peg people, wood pieces of various shapes, number cubes, clipboards, pencils, and paper, along with a coding board.

Figure 4.2. Sample Invitation for Learning: *Where Are You From?* by Yamile Saied Mendez

In the Invitation for Learning in figure 4.3, the book *We Sang You Home* by Richard Van Camp is offered alongside mirrors and materials such as a small disco ball, bells, bead necklaces, metal pieces, keys, peg people, and metal rods.

Figure 4.3. Sample Invitation for Learning: *We Sang You Home* by Richard Van Camp

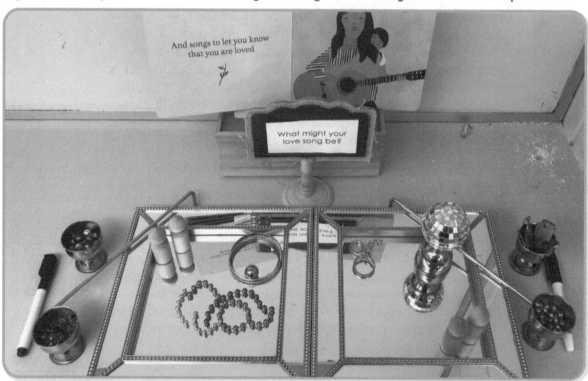

Additional samples of Invitations for Learning can be found in the Digital Resources (see page 219).

Like a gift, an Invitation for Learning is carefully thought out; the educator intentionally chooses each playful piece based on what is gathered about each child within the learning environment to appeal to children's interests. The educator's goal is to stimulate joy, wonder, excitement, and, ultimately, learning. The gift moves beyond its visual allure as every learner is invited to play while drawing on their cultural competencies and multiple intelligences. Each child is invited to make their mark in a unique way.

As children engage with an Invitation for Learning, they might reveal their divergent thinking or demonstrate a transference of skills. This informs the instructional moves that the educator needs to make next. The true gift lies within what learners say, do, or represent. The provocateur observes how the Invitation for Learning stimulates children's interests, thinking, and passions (Curtis and Carter 2017).

An Invitation for Learning

> → is responsive to learners' curiosities, interests, wonderings, and cultural currency;
>
> → motivates children to gain new competencies and provokes innovative insights through the materials presented;
>
> → connects to multiple learning outcomes and curriculum goals that are integrated into the experience;
>
> → evokes new content knowledge; and
>
> → provides multiple entry points for learners to demonstrate their thinking.

Preparing the Gift

> An invitation to learn is a display of materials, carefully selected and arranged, that draws children's attention and engages them in a world of wonder, exploration, and discovery. The invitation to learn is purposefully and intentionally designed with curriculum outcomes in mind. As the children interact with the invitation, the educator observes and documents the children's interests, thinking, and learning. The children's questions and interests can become the focus for an inquiry. (Curtis 2010, 1)

As you prepare to offer Invitations for Learning in your space, reflect on this definition and keep these principles in mind:

1. Present materials in aesthetically pleasing and orderly ways.

You should arrange the invitation in a way that entices children to enter play in a meaningful manner. Think about your own personal shopping experiences and how those spaces are organized to highlight specific items through aesthetically pleasing displays that capture your attention and appeal to your interests, needs, or desires. Similarly, Invitations for Learning should offer materials in ways that provide aesthetic appeal intertwined with intention and learning. Consider figures 4.4 and 4.5—which would you be more inclined to interact with?

Figure 4.4. A Carefully Designed Invitation for Learning

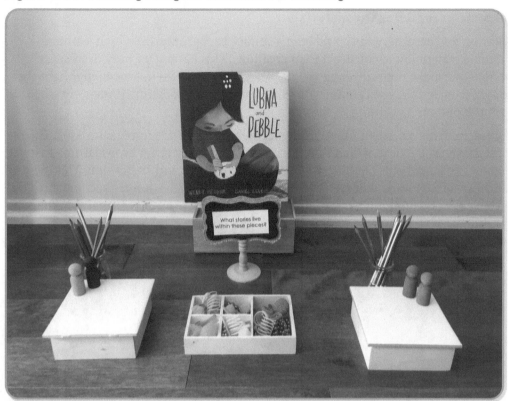

Figure 4.5. An Unplanned Learning Opportunity

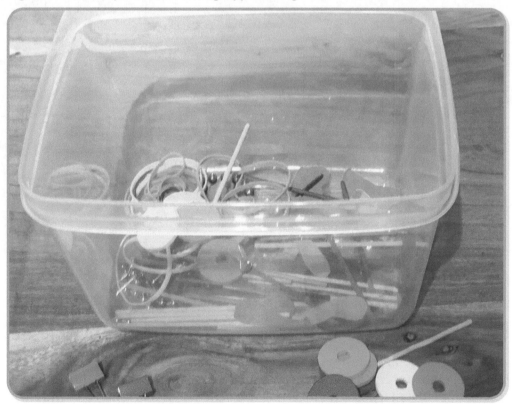

2. Offer a parameter for using the materials.

In an Invitation for Learning, you should offer a surface background on which learners can manipulate materials and construct their creations. This parameter provides a space where learners can make their thinking visible. It should be neutral in tone to highlight the properties of the materials; you can use wood slices, wicker mats, picture frames, tiles, boards, or other similar options.

The invitation in figure 4.6 uses a round mirror as the parameter. It presents the book *Shades of Me*, by Nadia Kenisha Bynoe, which shares the story of a young girl who is learning to love her skin color. Her sister helps her uncover the beauty that lives within her skin. This question is offered to learners: "How do you see yourself?" The book and question are accompanied by paintbrushes, dry-erase markers, permanent markers, peg people, multicultural skin-tone paint, and clipboards with paper.

Figure 4.6. An Invitation for Learning with a Mirror as the Parameter

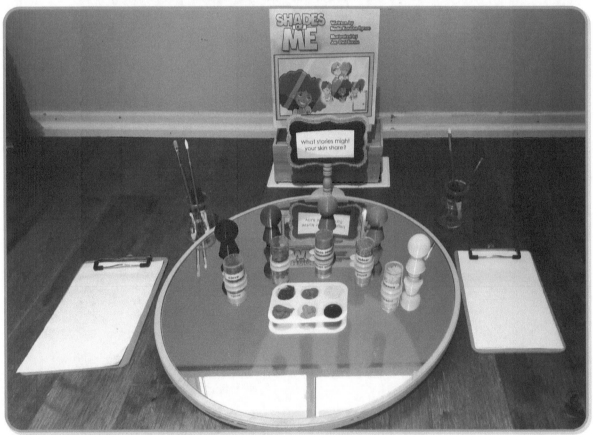

3. Present matching containers or baskets that are neutral in tone.

When you present materials in an invitation, house them in matching containers that draw children's attention to the properties of the materials. Neutral containers or baskets allow learners to focus on the contents instead of the container itself, drawing their attention to the color, size, shape, and texture of the items. If you instead offer materials in a brightly colored container, it may be difficult for learners to distinguish materials of that same color within the container (e.g., red items inside a red basket), and key properties can be camouflaged as a result. We should be purposeful in what we design; if an Invitation for Learning offers water, we should use transparent containers that allow learners to play and reveal properties such as sinking and floating, volume, cause and effect, and more.

4. **Highlight the materials' different attributes by grouping.**

You should group materials by color, size, shape, height, texture, and more to highlight their various properties. When you feature an attribute over time, you provoke learners to consider the different ways in which a particular material might be grouped or used. For example, you could sort blocks by color for a few weeks and observe learners who subsequently sort pieces by this property. Over time, you may choose to sort the blocks by size or shape instead to support learners in recognizing something new. Grouping provides opportunities for new perspectives on how materials can be used.

5. **Consider arrangements that highlight various sizes, scales, and levels.**

As you select materials and offer them to learners, capitalize on opportunities to highlight the sizes of materials. Consider the size of certain materials in relation to others. Scaling some of the playful pieces—for example, from smallest to largest—invites learners to problem-solve how the materials might be used in play. Also consider various levels of engagement. Learning does not live only at tables or desks; you can arrange invitations on the ground, on top of ledges, within shelving units, near windows, in cozy nooks, or under tables.

6. **Occasionally arrange materials to suggest possible outcomes for play.**

In Invitations for Learning, the playful pieces are arranged to inspire possible outcomes for the materials. We can support learners by providing ideas for how the materials can be manipulated. For example, an invitation could offer textiles from a specific culture and materials that elicit patterning. The educator could place a few loose parts to begin a pattern and provoke a child's thinking. Through this creation, the child may then notice and name patterns seen within the textile and make deeper connections in play.

7. **Reposition materials to spark new interest.**

Moving materials to different locations in the learning environment is a great way to stimulate new interests and ideas for learners as they build on their ideas. For instance, the educator could arrange loose parts in a container horizontally and then later reposition the materials vertically to provoke learners to consider using the playful pieces in a new way.

8. **Offer artifacts, visuals, or relevant text alongside loose parts.**

Using a text, an object, or a visual to anchor the Invitation for Learning sparks learners' interests and offers them a reference point for interacting with the materials. Intentionally placing them with loose parts feeds learners' curiosities in multiple ways.

What Are the Components of an Invitation for Learning?

Invitations for Learning reveal children's inner wonderings and desires and ultimately lead to inquiries and investigations that demonstrate their thinking over time. These foundational components should guide your thinking when designing an invitation:

→ Offer a book, an image, or an artifact that aligns with a conceptual understanding.

→ Offer an open-ended question.

→ Provide open-ended materials that can be used for a variety of purposes.

→ Provide a neutral background on which learners can use the materials.

→ Offer tools that provide more opportunities for learning and documentation.

Figure 4.7 illustrates these components in an invitation connected to the book *Love Is Love* by Michael Genhart. This text is about a boy who learns that love transcends gender, race, and sexual orientation; the book celebrates that the love shared within a family is real.

Figure 4.7. Components of an Invitation for Learning: *Love Is Love* by Michael Genhart

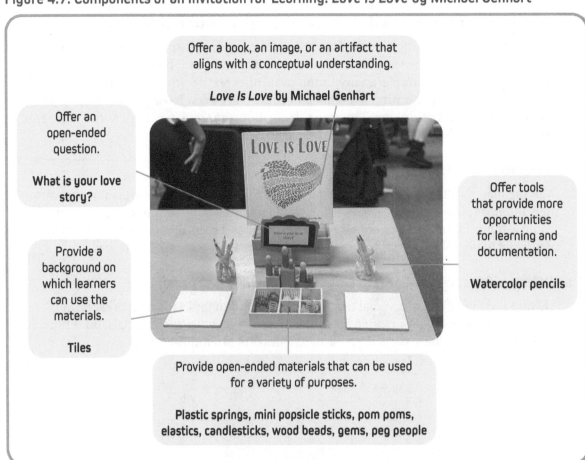

Offer a book, an image, or an artifact that aligns with a conceptual understanding.

***Love Is Love* by Michael Genhart**

Offer an open-ended question.

What is your love story?

Provide a background on which learners can use the materials.

Tiles

Offer tools that provide more opportunities for learning and documentation.

Watercolor pencils

Provide open-ended materials that can be used for a variety of purposes.

Plastic springs, mini popsicle sticks, pom poms, elastics, candlesticks, wood beads, gems, peg people

Figure 4.8 outlines the components of an invitation pairing metal bike figures and other materials with the book *Be a Maker* by Katey Howes. The text celebrates the creativity and design in our world, whether in musical rhythms, in artistic painting, or through design and invention of simple machines. The Digital Resources (see page 219) include additional examples demonstrating the components of an Invitation for Learning.

Figure 4.8. Components of an Invitation for Learning: *Be a Maker* by Katey Howes

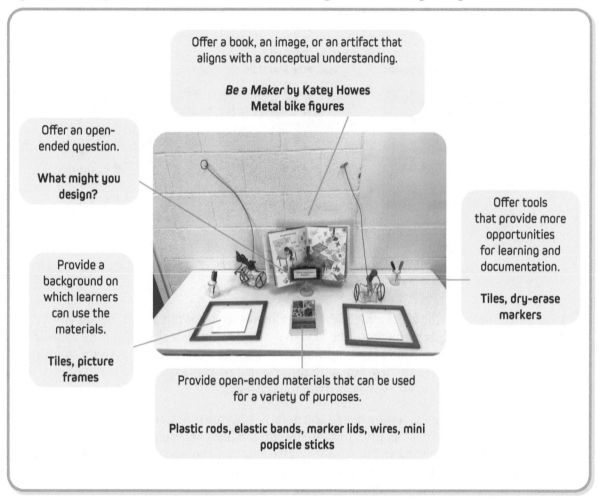

Offer a book, an image, or an artifact that aligns with a conceptual understanding.

**Be a Maker by Katey Howes
Metal bike figures**

Offer an open-ended question.

What might you design?

Provide a background on which learners can use the materials.

Tiles, picture frames

Offer tools that provide more opportunities for learning and documentation.

Tiles, dry-erase markers

Provide open-ended materials that can be used for a variety of purposes.

Plastic rods, elastic bands, marker lids, wires, mini popsicle sticks

Opportunities for Learning

We observe and plan appropriate learning experiences that support children's individual and collective needs. Three types of learning opportunities can be offered to learners: an activity, a provocation, and an Invitation for Learning (see figure 4.9).

Figure 4.9. Three Types of Learning Opportunities

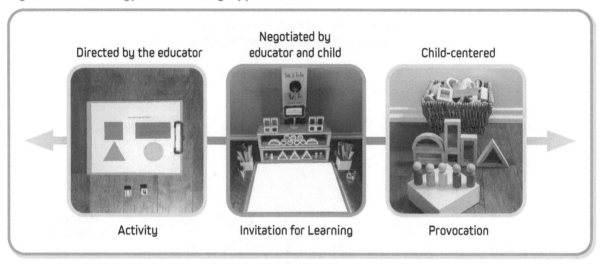

In an activity, the educator offers a high level of guidance to support learners' needs. For instance, at various points throughout the day, an educator notices a child skipping some letters when engaging with text within play. The educator responds by offering an activity to address this need one on one or in a small group with other learners. This experience is not offered to all learners, as it does not meet everyone's instructional needs.

An Invitation for Learning is responsive to learners' needs, one hundred languages, and strengths. The educator offers an invitation to deepen learning experiences and provide differentiation in an appealing and playful way. Learners can choose whether to interact with the invitation; through choice, each child has an opportunity to thrive in a space that honors the contributions they have made or intend to make.

The term *provocation* is often used interchangeably with *Invitation for Learning*; however, we believe there is a distinct difference between the two. An invitation might offer a text, a picture, or an artifact, along with a question that is paired with open-ended materials. It is intended to invite children to respond to what is offered. By contrast, a provocation offers an arrangement of open-ended materials to manipulate and tinker with. Children center their thinking around what is done with each playful piece. As provocateurs, we may observe what children do, say, and represent, then consider what book, artifact, or image and what question we can offer to spark deeper connections to the learning as it relates to curriculum. The provocation is meant to provoke thinking; it is not meant to steer the thought process with a question, book, image, or artifact. When we offer a question, an image, an artifact, or a text, we as the educator have directed the child's thinking to meet particular learning outcomes.

We believe that activities, Invitations for Learning, and provocations all serve a purpose. To truly honor children's capabilities and gifts, we provide opportunities for them to play with

Invitations for Learning and provocations, which allow them to deepen their thinking in ways that inspire possibility.

An activity

→ allows only one way or one method to engage in a task;

→ often has one desired outcome and does not allow divergent thinking;

→ is a teacher-directed experience where learners are expected to follow instructions;

→ leads to right and wrong learning outcomes;

→ is product-oriented; and

→ supports learners' specific needs that emerge based on assessments gathered.

An Invitation for Learning

→ is designed by the educator to intrigue learners or spark further exploration and investigation;

→ offers multiple entry points for learning and fosters divergent thinking;

→ gives choice to learners, as they are invited to accept the invitation that appeals to their interests;

→ is intentional and creates connections to the curriculum while also connecting to learners' interests and competencies;

→ honors the processes of thinking and learning;

→ may provoke an inquiry-worthy experience that can be explored over time;

→ supports a wide range of interests, strengths, and needs; and

→ informs next steps in planning and instruction.

A provocation

→ sparks interest and may create wonder, confusion, or even tension;

→ inspires reflection, deep thinking, conversations, and inquiries;

→ is led by children's thinking, as it does not include a text or a question;

→ may become an Invitation for Learning as the educator observes children's purpose and interest over time;

→ is fluid and can be transformed;

→ is centered around children's interests, strengths, and needs;

→ is open-ended and creative, with no right or wrong way to engage; and

→ supports planning for instructional moves.

Figure 4.10 illustrates these three types of learning opportunities.

Figure 4.10. Three Types of Learning Opportunities in Action

Activity	Invitation for Learning	Provocation

The educator offers this experience to learners in small-group instruction focused on meeting particular needs. To inform next steps for a learning experience, the educator observes what each child can do, can sometimes do, or has yet to do.	Based on learners' interactions with an activity and a provocation in a small-group setting, an Invitation for Learning emerges. Learners now have the opportunity to respond to a text, while the educator can observe how the learning has transferred from large- and small-group instruction to play.	The educator offers this provocation to provide multiple entry points for learners to demonstrate their thinking. Learners have autonomy in play and can choose to use the materials in the way that they desire.

How Should We Offer Invitations in Our Learning Spaces?

In the learning spaces that we create, we deliver invitations for children to play, investigate, and provoke with purpose. These spaces center children's beliefs and the one hundred languages that they speak.

→ **Consider offering multiple invitations that account for spacing within your learning environment and minimize clutter.** In chapter 2, we discussed the overwhelming feeling, or anesthetic effect, that children sometimes experience when too many materials are offered. There is no magic number; the number of offerings placed within the space is relative to learners' needs, interests, multiple intelligences, and competencies.

→ **Remember that your setup should not be predictable; instead, keep spaces fluid to keep learners intrigued by your offerings in various spaces.** When we invite possibilities, we encourage learners to think outside the box. We do not want to create conditions that are too predictable, which then result in experiences that are routine in thought.

→ **Prioritize balance.** Invitations for Learning should reflect balance by speaking to multiple languages and engaging multiple interests throughout the space. Balance is also present within an invitation's makeup. Figure 4.11 shows an example of the symmetrical placement of materials. This Invitation for Learning presents textile paper with patterns, along with this question: "What stories might you weave?" The materials include peg people, feathers, ribbon, elastic bands, wires, dry-erase markers, tiles, and a bamboo grid, all arranged in a symmetric, appealing way.

Figure 4.11. Balance in an Invitation for Learning

→ **Honor choice.** We should invite learners to choose where they would like to play as we facilitate and observe purposefully. Avoid creating rotation-based systems or structures that prohibit learners from revisiting Invitations for Learning or insisting that they explore all offerings within a specific time frame.

→ **Consider the gradients of sound and levels of invitations within your space.** An invitation that invites calm should be positioned in a space or area within the learning environment that is responsive to this intention; such an invitation should not be set in a high-traffic or high-volume area.

→ **Appeal to the senses and draw on the natural elements within the space.** As you consider where you will offer Invitations for Learning, consider how natural elements might create additional playful opportunities, such as natural light that might refract on the materials. Materials that create multisensory experiences (e.g., mirrored blocks) add new dimensions to play.

→ **Be intentional with the text that you offer.** When designing Invitations for Learning, it is important to elevate the text, as it should be highlighted and showcased for children to visit or revisit. You can also open the text to a particular page to elicit thinking around specific questions that are asked and yield higher possibilities with the playful materials.

→ **Carefully consider the sizing of containers.** Large bins or baskets of materials are not always necessary. Offering smaller containers gives learners the chance to problem-solve and use materials intentionally.

The Digital Resources (see page 219) include additional visual examples of how to offer Invitations for Learning.

Responsive Learning Opportunities

The open-ended nature of Invitations for Learning enables divergent thinking in action. When we invite learning, the gifts we offer prompt multiple responses that communicate learners' ideas. An activity, provocation, and Invitation for Learning have a symbiotic relationship (see figure 4.12). Through observations, we can gain insight into what a child always knows, sometimes knows, or has yet to know. This interdependence can manifest within a learning space in these ways:

→ Invitations for Learning and provocations may warrant independent activities to build skills that children need to develop.

→ Children may use specific materials at an Invitation for Learning, then move those items to another space where different loose parts are offered. The new interaction with these rearranged materials may inspire a provocation and uncover additional ways children may use the materials.

→ A provocation or Invitation for Learning might emerge from a response to an independent activity offered to a child one on one or in a small group.

→ A provocation may become an Invitation for Learning as children manipulate the loose parts. An interest may emerge that connects to a text, an image, an artifact, and/or a question.

We may gain insight into how children are able to transfer skills they learned from an activity during focused instruction to other Invitations for Learning or provocations within the space. Given the interdependence of the three types of opportunities, we suggest offering Invitations for Learning and provocations during exploration time. Activities focused on specific skills that learners are working to achieve are best offered in small groups or one on one. The information gathered through observations in multiple contexts (e.g., invitations, whole-group instruction, or small-group meetings) will inform what is offered and to whom within the flow of the learning day.

Figure 4.12. The Symbiotic Relationship of Different Learning Opportunities

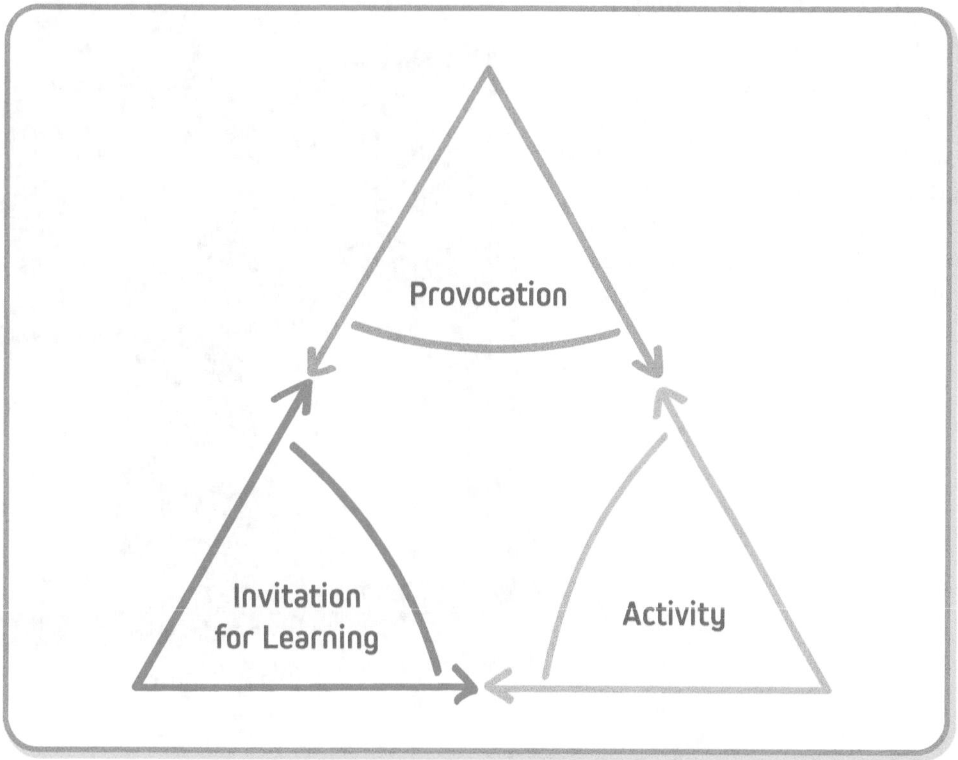

Identifying De-invitations

In some instances, what we perceive to be an Invitation for Learning might in fact be a misconception. When observed more carefully by the educator, it may not align with the components of an invitation and may instead be a *de-invitation*. While such a learning experience might be well intentioned, its impact often detracts from the potential learning outcomes. The de-invitation is no longer yielding the best possible outcome for thinking and knowledge building. Creating beautiful arrangements that captivate learners and spark curiosities goes beyond the realm of "pretty pedagogy." When a focus on beauty outshines and overrides the intention, we devalue the optimal learning that can be achieved through play, resulting in a de-invitation. A de-invitation is a misconception in an arrangement of an invitation by the educator. This is not to be confused with a missed invitation, which refers to missed opportunities in learning and teaching. You may identify many misconceptions that live within de-invitations.

The following pages show the most prevalent types of de-invitations, based on our own observations and experiences. While the books shown may provide excellent learning opportunities, in these examples the offerings do not align with the components of an invitation for learning.

Types of De-Invitations

1. **Materials Mismatch: The materials do not align with the expectations, goals, and/or schemas of play.**

   Figure 4.13 shows a setup with a prompt that invites learners to build. As we observe the materials, we notice that wood geoboards are offered; these materials do not allow for three-dimensional play. Instead, they limit the potential for children to create complex structures that are vertical and three-dimensional.

Figure 4.13. Materials Mismatch

Figure 4.14. Playsheet

2. **Playsheet: The learning outcome is limited to one answer, so it is predetermined; the learning opportunity serves as a living worksheet.**

   The de-invitation shown in figure 4.14 offers a specific collection of letters that learners are asked to match. With these materials, learners have limited opportunities to show their thinking beyond what is asked of them.

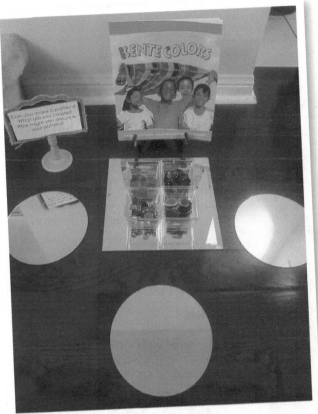

Figure 4.15. Question Conundrum

3. **Question Conundrum: The question is not open-ended, the question operates as a command (e.g., "Can you make a pattern?"), or multiple questions are asked (e.g., "How might you build a structure? What materials can you use? What is your plan?").**

The learning opportunity shown in figure 4.15 offers multiple questions for children to consider ("Can you make a pattern? What did you create? How might you describe your pattern?"). Multiple questions can be overwhelming for learners. One of the questions also commands learners to create something specific, which limits their opportunity to demonstrate thinking beyond the creation of a pattern. The inquiry is imposed on learners, and the ownership of the question lies with the educator, as opposed to the child.

4. **Main Idea Mayhem: The main idea of the text does not connect to the question or materials being offered.**

The text shown in figure 4.16 includes beautiful artwork and honors the stories of refugees who have escaped civil war to find refuge in new lands; however, the question paired with the book invites learners to stack rocks to create an inukshuk (a stone structure built and used by Indigenous peoples of the Arctic regions of North America). The disconnect between the text and the question represents a missed opportunity for learners to make deeper connections with the text and represent their thinking and understanding. We also question the intention in offering rocks to recreate an inukshuk as it is a misrepresentation of inuksuit (plural for *inukshuk*). There are many types of inuksuit. We question what prior knowledge has been uncovered in partnership with Indigenous community members prior to offering this. It is important to give the context of Inuit culture. For example, the educator may consider using the text *A Walk on the Tundra* by Rebecca Hainnu.

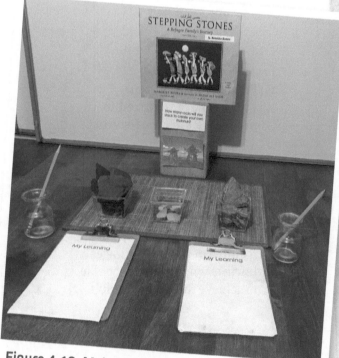

Figure 4.16. Main Idea Mayhem

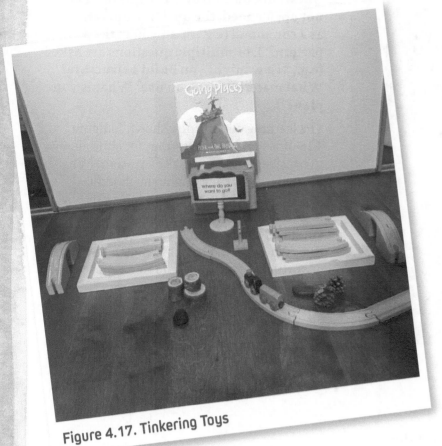

Figure 4.17. Tinkering Toys

5. **Tinkering Toys: The materials offered are not open-ended; they incorporate toys that have predetermined outcomes.**

Offering toys that are specific in their function and marketed in particular ways prohibits learners from forming their own theories and connections with the materials. The learning opportunity shown in figure 4.17 offers trains and train tracks for learners to play with. While learners might be able to share their ideas through this experience, their play will likely center around the topic of trains. When we design our Invitations for Learning, we should instead offer children open-ended materials that can be played with in multiple ways.

6. **Product Production: Learners are required to produce a specific product.**

As shown in figure 4.18, when we ask learners to create a specific product (in this case, a friendship bracelet), we limit their creative potential. Indicating to learners what is required of them discourages learners who might not be able to achieve the required result.

Figure 4.18. Product Production

7. **Supply Scarcity: Only one open-ended material is offered, and possibilities for play are limited.**

   Providing a limited number of playful pieces does not invite learners to problem-solve, innovate, or deepen their thinking. The learning opportunity pictured in figure 4.19 presents Haikubes (cubes with words written on them) that can be used to create a message. Some children may share words they feel connected to, while other learners may disengage from this de-invitation because they feel restricted by the words in the container. Offering learners such limited materials narrows their ability to represent ideas in various ways.

Figure 4.19. Supply Scarcity

Figure 4.20. Colossal Confusion

8. **Colossal Confusion: An abundance of materials makes it difficult for learners to decipher the items and use them in intentional ways.**

   Offering an array of materials is important; however, when too many are presented (as in figure 4.20), learners become overwhelmed and confused, and they misuse the materials because they are unsure of how to use the pieces in purposeful ways. We suggest instead reducing the number of materials to avoid shutting down learners' senses; working with a more manageable number also allows learners to make deeper connections to the items.

Types of De-Invitations (continued)

9. **Fake Fallacy: A learning opportunity with artificial materials limits authentic exploration of living things.**

   Offering certain materials that are synthetic (such as the artificial flower shown in figure 4.21 or plastic worms placed in soil) provides minimal opportunity for learners to investigate and explore properties of growth and decay. Learners make little connection to things that are not authentically experienced; thus, these items do not enrich the learning process. When children manipulate objects that cannot change over time, they miss out on the opportunity to build an understanding of the life cycle and our responsibility to care for living things.

Figure 4.21. Fake Fallacy

Interacting with Invitations for Learning is like the experience of receiving a gift. Anticipation and excitement build as you begin to unwrap the contents. As more of the gift is revealed, you gain deeper connections to the contents and what is revealed in the process of opening the package. For children to pursue the gifts we offer, we must plan and design thoughtful experiences that allow learners to respond to, challenge, and extend learning. In chapter 5, we continue this journey by exploring planning with purpose, which ensures that our Invitations for Learning yield optimal learning through play.

Additional Considerations

Missed Invitations

Invitations for Learning drive purpose in play while integrating curriculum outcomes that foster successful learning experiences. As we honor the gifts that these learning experiences present to children and educators, we also need to be mindful to not deviate from the intentions offered by learning opportunities. Here we share some common misconceptions that we might encounter:

Missed Invitation 1: Invitations for Learning should be modeled by the educator or include steps to instruct learners on how to play.

Too often, children are expected to do what is asked of them by the educator. Educators might want to drive the learning and steer the thinking of children. If we do not relinquish the learning to children in collaborative ways, we run the risk of doing the play *for* our learners. Dictating what should and should not happen in play leads to narrow outcomes for learning and assessment that depend on one result, which does not suit all learners' needs. Play "is also a reminder that passive approaches such as seat work, worksheets, scripted programs, and rote learning are antithetical to play-based paradigms for learning" (Singh and Brownell 2019, 2). In the early years, our focus is on the *process* of thinking that leads to growth and development. The goal of learning is not the product itself; instead, it is the learning that has occurred in achieving the end product.

Missed Invitation 2: Learners should rotate through a series of Invitations for Learning.

When we offer Invitations for Learning, we need to allow learners to choose what they want to engage with. When learners lack choice, they become dependent on what the educator determines is best for them. If we instead honor children as competent beings, we follow their lead as they choose to enter play where they feel most invited. The offering that draws on their interests can be transformed over time into new experiences that will build on their prior knowledge or challenge their thinking in new ways.

Missed Invitation 3: Invitations for Learning should be changed weekly.

Making changes to Invitations for Learning on a weekly basis limits opportunities for learners to communicate their thoughts and ideas over time. When learners have multiple opportunities to engage with materials, they develop ongoing relationships with the materials that reveal their growth in learning; the educator can gain key insights from observing how these relationships take shape. Changing learning opportunities too quickly also prohibits some learners from having the chance to interact with a particular Invitation for Learning. The frequency of the changes made to the learning environment should be informed by what learners reveal through their interactions in the space. Making too many shifts too quickly does not support the process required for learners to make deep and meaningful connections to the gifts offered to them.

Missed Invitation 4: Children must visit all Invitations for Learning in the learning space.

We highlight once again the importance of choice in play. Children should not be directed to particular Invitations for Learning, as there is no formula for their navigation of learning. As educators, we must be open to observe, listen to, and respond to what our learners communicate in their desired areas of play. We then can consider what materials, books, or questions we may want to offer next to spark new learning.

Missed Invitation 5: Invitations for Learning should be put out when children are ready to engage with them, not at the beginning of the year.

Learners are always ready to communicate through the one hundred languages. We must invite possibilities for these languages to be spoken at every moment of the day, week, or year. As educators, we must be ready to document the journey as learners build relationships with and connections to the Invitations for Learning over time. We can then leverage our observations and co-construct conditions for learning that will support all children in successfully navigating Invitations for Learning throughout the space over time.

Missed Invitation 6: All provocations become Invitations for Learning.

Provocations are a great way to invite learners to interact with materials as we observe them and consider changes for learning. We have already shared that provocations can become Invitations for Learning, but this is not always the case. Provocations can also inspire educators to add elements *within* an Invitation for Learning; these materials may shift over time but still remain a provocation in and of itself.

Unraveling the Knots

Invitations for Learning encourage children's gifts to be revealed; they invite differentiation using play-based approaches to learning. Children's inner thoughts and processes are uncovered as connections are made to learning goals and curriculum standards. As we pursue the gift of offering Invitations for Learning, we need to be cognizant of the knots that can entangle us along the way:

Knot 1: Beauty should be prioritized when offering an Invitation for Learning.

When an invitation focuses on beauty, materials, and arrangement but lacks intention or connection to learning, we refer to it as "pretty pedagogy." Learners, their interests, and their needs must remain the central driving force for the invitations that we offer within our spaces. Children need to be captivated by the arrangements in ways that focus on the learning. When the aesthetic is prioritized, a miscommunication of intention will occur, and we will miss the opportunity to capture learners' insight and knowledge. When arrangements focus heavily on beauty, learners often view the invitation not as a place for interaction but rather as one to simply observe. An Invitation for Learning should market learning and entice children to interact in meaningful ways.

Knot 2: "Real" work at tables must be completed before children venture to Invitations for Learning.

This concept supports the idea that work is to be completed before the reward of play is given. As educators, we have inherited legacies that seat work and the filling out of worksheets constitute the consolidation of learning and skills. We must shift this antiquated way of thinking, as play provides opportunities for learners to articulate their ideas in ways that are developmentally appropriate and meaningful to them. As we have shared in the previous chapters, play *is* the work of a child. Consequently, Invitations for Learning should not live in isolation among other activities.

Knot 3: Invitations for Learning should be created around a central theme.

We have observed that children who engage with Invitations for Learning focused on a central theme (e.g., autumn) may be stifled in thinking beyond the object, topic, or theme. The theme becomes the driving force, and play centers around this concept. While this theme may capture children's interest, focusing on it does not maximize the learning potential. In addition, these themes are often marketed to specific audiences and particular social identities. The learning then becomes isolated and may generate tension for learners whose ideas are not honored in open-ended ways.

Pursuing the Gift

As you begin your journey in offering learning opportunities, remember to make small shifts that invite learning through play. These moves will help you along the way:

→ **Start simply.** Now that you have gathered a collection of loose parts for your space, consider pairing them with an artifact, a text, a textile, or a photo, along with a question. Or consider offering a few provocations within your space, and observe how learners use the materials; this can help you determine whether a particular provocation could evolve into an Invitation for Learning.

→ **Shake things up!** If you already offer centers or activities in your learning environment, consider what elements you can add, change, or extend to create an Invitation for Learning that broadens the learning experience.

→ **Focus on the familiar.** Consider offering Invitations for Learning with books you are already planning on reading and using with learners, or books you know well and can easily make playful connections to.

Gifts of Learning

Children experience the gifts of learning as they engage in play through Invitations for Learning. To summarize the key concepts explored in this chapter:

→ An Invitation for Learning is a beautiful arrangement of playful pieces that are intentionally chosen to provoke children's curiosity as they make connections and discoveries to enhance their understanding of the world.

→ The true gift of an Invitation for Learning comes from what learners say, do, or represent, which informs the educator's next instructional moves.

→ An Invitation for Learning should include these components: a book, an image, or an artifact that aligns with a conceptual understanding; an open-ended question; open-ended materials that can be used for a variety of purposes; a background on which learners can use the materials; and tools that provide more opportunities for learning and documentation.

→ There are three types of learning opportunities, which serve different purposes: activities, provocations, and Invitations for Learning.

→ We need to consider the elements when offering Invitations for Learning to ensure that we are creating a space that speaks.

→ De-invitations can resemble Invitations for Learning, but present issues that detract from learning.

As we highlight the important ideas read in this chapter, we urge you to offer learning opportunities that center learning. We offer these questions for reflection to support you in your pursuits:

→ What Invitations for Learning might you offer that honor children's interests, identities, and learning needs?

→ How might you prioritize a variety of learning opportunities in your environment?

→ How might you ensure that the components of Invitations for Learning are honored?

Michael Hall

Red

A Crayon's Story

What? Uh-oh.

How might you help
Red?

Chapter 5
Planning with Purpose

The manner of giving is worth more than the gift.

—*Pierre Corneille*

A true gift is reciprocal in nature; it allows for a transference of expression and joy. When we present learners with Invitations for Learning, we are deliberate in what we select and offer, as we want to evoke delight for the children receiving the gift. A gift offered with purpose is responsive to learners' needs, strengths, and abilities. When learners receive such a gift, they in turn offer the educator moments of joy, new learning, and an application of skills acquired.

The Gift That Keeps on Giving

As we prepare to offer gifts to learners, our planning and intention should focus on the recipients of the gifts. Children in our spaces possess a diverse range of strengths, interests, and needs. Our offerings must appeal to learners in engaging and sustainable ways. We should see our Invitations for Learning as the gifts that keep on giving. Take a look at the learning opportunities shown in figures 5.1 and 5.2.

→ In each opportunity, whose strengths are honored or dishonored?

→ Which opportunity yields more possibilities?

→ Which opportunity would captivate and sustain learners' interests over time?

Figure 5.1. A Worksheet about *Red: A Crayon's Story*

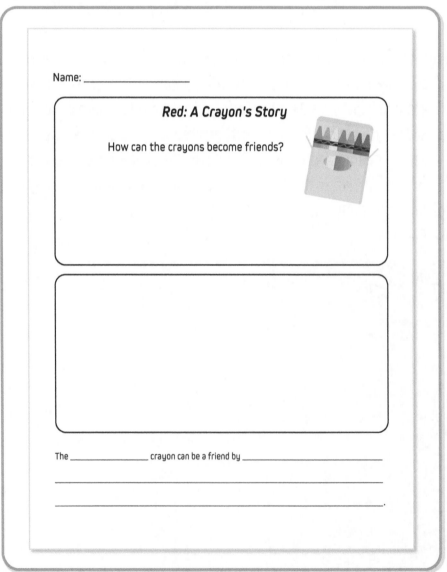

Figure 5.2. An Invitation for Learning Connected to *Red: A Crayon's Story*

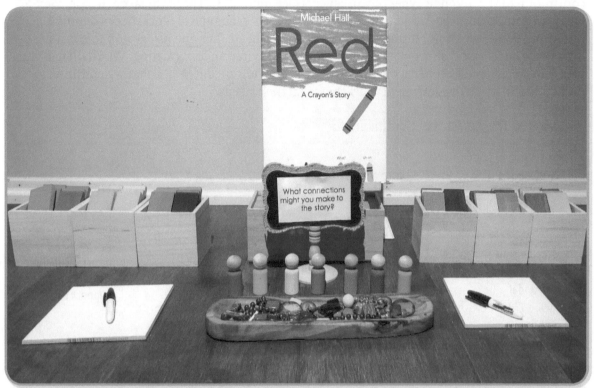

The worksheet (figure 5.1) isolates skills and limits learners' potential to express themselves in multiple ways. For example, in figure 5.1, children are limited to drawing a picture and answering the question as prompted and guided by what is written on the page. This experience is narrow in focus and does not align with multiple expectations or differentiate to meet learners' particular needs. The Invitation for Learning (figure 5.2) invites learners to represent their thinking in various ways. It provides multiple access points for curriculum and learning to address different learners' needs, wants, and interests. The open question paired with open-ended materials offers learners opportunities to respond in multiple ways. The invitation honors choice, and learners' responses to the question may differ based on how they use the open-ended materials. In this invitation for learning, the children may respond through writing or engage in mathematical thinking through the use of the blocks; they may also demonstrate their understanding of the story by using the materials to retell and so much more. "Generic language activities—for example, having children complete worksheets—should be avoided: they are rarely effective because their focus is narrow and they provide limited assessment information about the child's level of understanding" (Ontario Ministry of Education 2016b, 72).

To create spaces that speak, we must invest in sustainable learning habits that nourish children's thoughts. We need to establish an environment that supports a *culture of thinking*, where learners problem-solve their way to new ideas, instead of a *culture of doing*, where learners passively create products. Learning opportunities should always support process-oriented outcomes that value children's thinking and learning. When we gift offerings that are responsive to learners' many languages, we amplify the voices of all children. Educators who respect learners' strengths and needs prioritize goals, build on existing knowledge, and plan intentionally for instruction through differentiated opportunities.

Jennifer Gonzalez (2018) shares that "not all worksheets are created equal"; she has created a continuum of the different types of worksheets (see figure 5.3). There are layers to consider when offering a worksheet, and this continuum reveals each type of worksheet's depth of intention. While we do not dismiss the use of "powersheets," we encourage you to consider how using such a worksheet would complement an Invitation for Learning. We challenge you to rethink the worksheet pedagogy that speaks to the inherited legacies that we continue to perpetuate, often to the detriment of learners and their needs.

Figure 5.3. The Worksheet Continuum

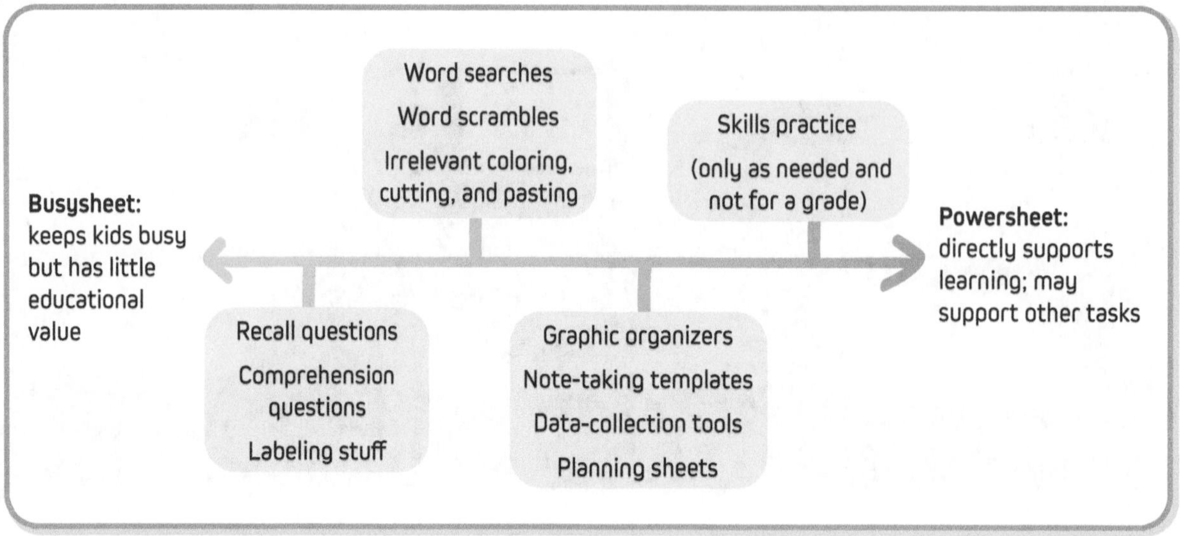

Source: Gonzalez (2018)

To create Invitations for Learning that are true gifts for learners, you must plan with purpose, as outlined below. Let's explore each step of this process in more detail.

Follow Learners' Interests

→ Determine learners' interests.

→ Consider their identities and lived experiences.

→ Consider big ideas and conceptual understandings.

Select a Text, a Photo, or an Artifact, and Connect It to the Curriculum

→ Select a text, a photo, or an artifact (physical or digital) that will resonate with learners.

→ Identify learning goals and curriculum expectations.

→ Consider how the chosen text, photo, or artifact supports learners' strengths, needs, interests, identities, and lived experiences.

Develop a Question

→ Is the question open-ended?

→ Does it offer multiple possibilities for play and learning?

→ How will the question provoke learners to think in various ways?

→ Does the question align with the text and the curriculum expectations?

Consider the Materials

→ Are the materials open-ended?

→ Which schemas will align with the materials?

→ How do the materials connect to the question you are asking?

Organize and Market

→ How will you organize the materials?

→ What parameters will you establish for play?

→ Identify a space within the environment where you can offer the Invitation for Learning.

→ How will you market the materials to entice learners to engage with them?

Assess and Reflect

→ Document how learners interact with the Invitation for Learning.

→ Reflect on how learners have engaged with the materials.

→ Consider what may need to be revised or reconsidered within the Invitation for Learning.

Follow Learners' Interests

We look to children for guidance on how best to plan and prepare Invitations for Learning that will sustain their interests over time. Invitations for Learning are responsive offerings that emerge from our observations of children. "They are the plans formed as a result of synthesizing the many ideas you generate about children's theories and ways to plan curriculum that can help children explore their ideas more deeply" (Broderick and Hong 2020, 29).

A differentiated approach to learning is adopted when planning Invitations for Learning, as we draw near to the various learning styles that support children in their acquisition of knowledge (Tomlinson 2017). Differentiated planning requires a firm understanding of learners' strengths, interests, and development to provide multiple pathways of learning (Tomlinson 2017).

We create multiple pathways for learning when differentiated planning involves three elements: (1) content, (2) process, and (3) demonstrations of learning (Tomlinson 2017). We must ensure that learners are offered rigorous *content* programming that responds to, challenges, and extends thinking through student-centered opportunities. This involves a reflective *process* where we as educators have a strong understanding of self and reflect on our preferences; we must consider how our own preferences may be imposed on learners, disguised as their own. As we reflect, we consider learners and hold high expectations of them to inform our planning. Learners' cultures will guide our way, with the development of their cultural competence as our compass for planning and programming. Learning experiences must offer children opportunities to *demonstrate* their thinking and learning in multiple ways.

As you seek to follow children's interests when planning Invitations for Learning, consider these questions:

→ How can your observations reveal learners' interests?

→ How do you know these are the interests of the children?

→ How can you confirm your understanding based on documentation in collaboration with another educator?

→ How can your planning consider children's learning styles and incorporate the one hundred languages?

→ How do learners' interests align with their needs, the learning goals, and the curriculum?

Select a Text, a Photo, or an Artifact, and Connect It to the Curriculum

Texts can honor learners' lived experiences based on connections and commonalities or provide windows into others' experiences. Books allow readers the opportunity to center their own identities while exploring a world beyond their own perspectives. When books serve as windows, they have the power to shift ideas, transform thinking, and build on learners' schema (Bishop 1990). Books are powerful tools that provide entry points for learners to understand their own identities and how they may interact and intersect on a global scale.

Pairing an Invitation for Learning with a text provides the educator with the opportunity to discuss who matters, who is important, whose voices are heard and whose are silenced, and who is visible and who is not. We must remember that what children don't see speaks just as loudly as what they do see (Derman-Sparks and Edwards 2020). As educators, we must be critical and intentional about the ways we use text in our learning environments. It is vital that we reflect on our own identities and how they influence which texts we select, as well as how we use our identities to enhance culturally relevant conversations. Revisit the tenet of critical

Playful Note

When considering a text, you can document themes and big ideas or concepts that emerge from the text with sticky notes. You can also partner with a colleague, critical friend, or division team to analyze the text and document themes together as a way to gather multiple perspectives.

consciousness discussed in chapter 1; as you select texts, consider how they can be anchored for critical dialogue to deepen relationships with social advocacy and justice.

When planning an Invitation for Learning, we must also reconsider what can be defined as a text. In Invitations for Learning, text can also take the form of photographs, magazines, posters, song lyrics, QR codes that link to videos or songs, poetry, newspapers, recipes, and more. A picture speaks one thousand words, and through the one hundred languages these words can be amplified when they are gifted within an Invitation for Learning. Challenging notions of what qualifies as a text allows learners to harness the multiple literacies that exist and can be critically revolutionary for early learners. The Digital Resources (page 219) include examples of a variety of texts that you can offer in an Invitation for Learning.

After considering a text and learners' interests, we need to remember that curriculum is at the core of our offerings. Learning opportunities that do not invite children to explore learning goals and address needs simply remain beautiful offerings that perpetuate pretty pedagogy. As you plan Invitations for Learning, consult with your district's or school board's curriculum and/or learning expectations. Our responsibility as educators is to ensure that we weave the curriculum into the play opportunities that we present to our learners in an integrated fashion. Play should invite the curriculum to thrive, and once we have designed the experience, its benefits become illuminating for learners, their families, and ourselves as educators.

As you select text for Invitations for Learning, reflect on these questions:

- → What interests, identities, and lived experiences support your selection of the text? How can the text leverage the curriculum in integrated ways?

- → What types of text appeal to learners?

- → How can the text connect to multiple learning goals or curriculum expectations?

- → How can the text support multiple learning contexts (large-group, small-group, and focused instruction)?

Develop a Question

A question frames experiences in play and adds great depth to an Invitation for Learning; it provokes thinking, initiates conversation, and invites pedagogical pivots for children. Educators are provocateurs who creatively invite learners to summon their own ideas, theories, and curiosities through a question. The way you frame a question can open up experiences for playful investigation to thrive.

Playful Note

As you review the documentation you have collected, highlight the interests that overlap, are trending, or continuously emerge. You can use sticky notes for documentation and group them to create a visual map of key ideas and interests. You can also use digital applications where categories or labels can be attached to documentation for later sorting (e.g., Google Keep).

Questions can

→ prompt learning, inquiry, and curiosity;

→ cultivate academic rigor and promote critical evaluation;

→ provide entry points for assessment; and

→ provoke dialogue and inform inquiry within the learning environment.

Figure 5.4 presents the fundamentals of questioning based on Bloom's taxonomy.

Figure 5.4. Fundamentals of Questioning

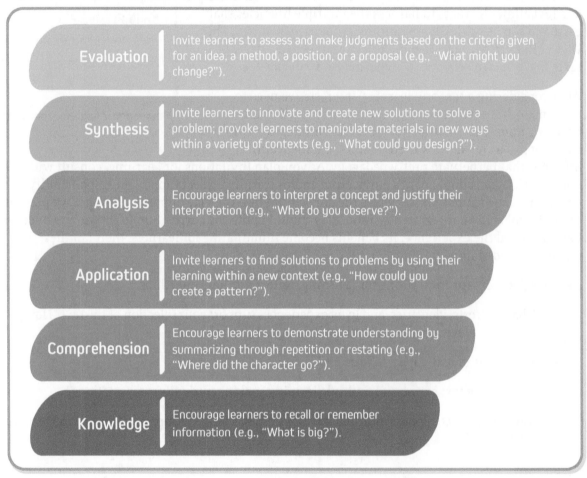

Evaluation — Invite learners to assess and make judgments based on the criteria given for an idea, a method, a position, or a proposal (e.g., "What might you change?").

Synthesis — Invite learners to innovate and create new solutions to solve a problem; provoke learners to manipulate materials in new ways within a variety of contexts (e.g., "What could you design?").

Analysis — Encourage learners to interpret a concept and justify their interpretation (e.g., "What do you observe?").

Application — Invite learners to find solutions to problems by using their learning within a new context (e.g., "How could you create a pattern?").

Comprehension — Encourage learners to demonstrate understanding by summarizing through repetition or restating (e.g., "Where did the character go?").

Knowledge — Encourage learners to recall or remember information (e.g., "What is big?").

Source: Adapted from Cline (n.d.).

When we craft questions that provoke with purpose, we invite strategies that foster a culture of inquiry. These guidelines can support you in developing a good question:

→ Consider what you know about learners and possible responses they may give.

→ Reflect on how your question offers opportunities for curriculum or learning goals to emerge.

- → Ensure that your question is open-ended and provides multiple entry points for thinking.

- → Pose a question that elicits higher levels of cognitive skills as defined in Bloom's taxonomy.

- → Ask a question that opens up opportunities for diverse perspectives to be expressed.

- → The role of the question is to provoke and to give learners an opportunity to respond in the language that they speak best. In the article "Asking Effective Questions," Brandon Cline shares the power of a good question and what results it can yield:

  > While asking questions may seem a simple task, it is perhaps the most powerful tool we possess as teachers. If we ask the right question of the right student at the right moment, we may inspire her to new heights of vision and insight. A good question can excite, disturb, or comfort, and eventually yield an unexpected bounty of understanding and critical awareness. But even apart from such serendipitous moments, question-asking serves many functions that make it the stock in trade of the skillful teacher. (Cline, n.d., para. 1)

If you need a tool to support you in crafting questions for your Invitations for Learning, consider using a Q chart (see figure 5.5). Consider where your question sits on the chart. Can it elicit opportunities for application, evaluation, creation, or analysis?

Figure 5.5. Q Chart

	what	where/ when	which	who	why	how
is						
did/does/ do	remembering and understanding			understanding and applying		
can						
could						
will/would	applying, analyzing, and creating			evaluating, analyzing, and creating		
might						

Consider the Materials

A harmonious relationship emerges when we pair loose parts with a provocative question and an appropriate text or artifact. The Invitations for Learning that we deliver are beautiful presents. They are wrapped with intention and care, but the content is only as good as its pieces. As you read in chapter 3, open-ended materials unleash divergent thinking and learning. Multiple pathways and access points are offered when we are selective in choosing loose parts. "Learning is creation, not consumption. Knowledge is not something a learner absorbs but something a learner creates" (Couros 2016, para. 16).

For children to create and take ownership of their learning, we must gift them with the tools necessary to achieve new understandings. As noted in chapter 3, there are seven types of loose parts that engage learners in play:

- → Nature-based
- → Wood reuse
- → Plastic
- → Ceramic and glass
- → Fabric and ribbon
- → Packaging
- → Metal

Loose parts are a gateway to divergent play. To enact such rich experiences, you should share playful pieces that are diverse and lead to multiple outcomes.

Figure 5.6 shows an example of a virtual Invitation for Learning connected to the text *Malaika's Costume*. This book is about a young girl who is preparing for Carnival by gathering materials to create a costume. Her grandmother helps her design a peacock costume to dance in the parade. The Invitation for Learning offers swatches of fabric, ribbons, feathers, gems in various shapes, bead necklaces, and mannequins, along with the question "What might you design?" Learners are invited to be innovative and create their own designs by using Google Slides. Children can engage with this experience independently or play virtually with a peer. They can create costumes, headpieces, or outfits that might be worn. They can also compare the sizes of their creations with others. Some children may choose to design parade floats or decorate the space to create the setting of the story. Learners can also explore and create patterns using the virtual materials offered, engage in sharing stories connected to their own experiences, or retell the text.

When planning Invitations for Learning, you should also consider using artifacts in addition to loose parts. Artifacts such as musical instruments, textiles, natural structures, and items of cultural significance present learning opportunities that are responsive to learners' identities, extend thinking, and challenge normative understandings. Gifting artifacts requires intentional planning; you should consult with children, families, and communities to ensure that what is shared as an artifact is respected and does not misappropriate or misrepresent a culture. The Digital Resources (page 219) provide examples of how to use artifacts in Invitations for Learning.

Playful Note

It is possible to offer loose parts when learning virtually. You can take photos of playful pieces or use clip art images with transparent backgrounds. These virtual loose parts can be offered in apps such as Google Slides or Google Jamboard where children can move and manipulate the materials.

Figure 5.6. A Virtual Invitation for Learning Connected to *Malaika's Costume*

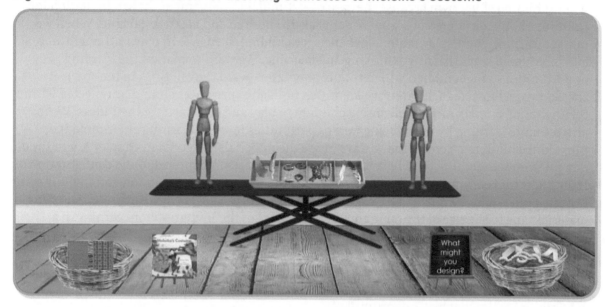

Play remains the vehicle for learning in our spaces that speak; we think of the materials we offer as the engine that drives learners to share their thinking and learning. Our selection of materials must be intentional, reflective, and provocative. As you consider what materials to offer in Invitations for Learning, ask yourself these questions:

→ Are the materials open-ended?

→ How can you include culturally relevant materials to provoke thinking?

→ How do the materials align with schemas?

→ How do the materials offer sensory experiences for learners?

→ How do the materials connect to the question you are asking?

→ Would the quantity of materials offered allow for problem solving and innovation?

Organize and Market

Invitations for Learning are organized with the intention to market them in a way that provokes and promotes thinking. When designing an invitation, we should consider how the materials are positioned. If we want to draw learners' attention to the ideas and concepts within a book, the book should be a focal point. This can be done by presenting the book in an elevated position (e.g., on a stand in the middle of the invitation). The question should be positioned in a manner that invites inquiry around the conceptual understanding we want learners to examine. An array of playful pieces can be offered in neutral containers that highlight the attributes of the materials. If a container is the same color as the contents, the materials become camouflaged, and it may become difficult for children to notice the materials' attributes.

Our simple message to you is that less is more. Visual clutter leads to an anesthetic response, where children shut down because they are overstimulated. Remember that an Invitation for Learning should be offered in a way that appeals to children and *markets* learning. When we market learning, we display materials that entice children to engage in play in thoughtful and intentional ways that drive thinking and learning. We want to market the learning opportunities so that children will naturally gravitate toward the offerings in the space. It should not feel forced; their interests, identities, or lived experiences should be reflected within the Invitations for Learning, welcoming children to play and demonstrate their ideas. We may also promote learning by introducing new opportunities into the learning environment or provoking children to consider new ways to use the materials. As noted in chapter 4, you should aim for symmetry, scaling, and balance. This concept can also be applied to the configuration of Invitations for Learning on tables that are large in dimension. Figure 5.7 shows an Invitation for Learning offered in the middle of a large table. In this setup, learners have difficulty accessing materials due to the size of the table and the placement of the Invitation for Learning. If a child is reaching for the materials and having a hard time accessing them, we can instead offer two different invitations on the same table, as shown in figure 5.8. In this setup, the educator maximizes the learning space by moving the original invitation to one end of the table and offering another invitation on the other side of the table. This arrangement allows for more accessibility and richer play opportunities.

Figure 5.7. A Single Invitation for Learning on a Large Table

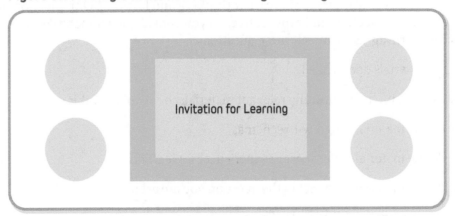

Figure 5.8. Two Invitations for Learning on a Large Table

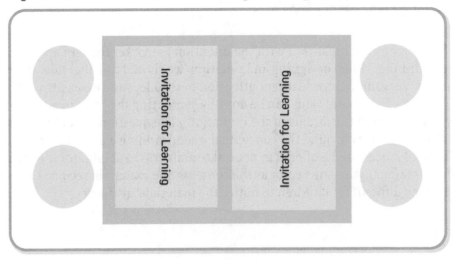

The elements within an Invitation for Learning can be configured in multiple ways. A shift in configuration is a provocation in itself, and it provides new perspective and insight for learners who interact with the invitation. When considering the arrangement of your Invitations for Learning, ask yourself these questions:

→ How can the materials be organized?

→ What parameters will you establish for play? (Consider accessibility, scaling, and the way the materials will be grouped.) Remember that the parameter itself might be used by learners as a material; it, too, should be moveable and flexible.

→ How can you market the materials to entice and provoke learners? Would it invite and inspire you to play? Does the Invitation for Learning speak to multiple learners through the one hundred languages?

→ How can you offer the materials to highlight particular attributes? Consider diversity, texture, sound, smell, and color.

→ Where can you gift the Invitation for Learning within the space to invite optimal interaction?

Assess and Reflect

Once we offer an Invitation for Learning within the space, we observe, assess, and reflect on how learners interact with the materials, each other, and the environment to consider possible next steps and new outcomes. We delve further into pedagogical documentation and play in chapter 6, "Playful Assessments." We've provided a planning template (figure 5.9) and a self-reflection tool (figure 5.10) with questions to use when developing Invitations for Learning.

A Call to Action

The following scenario illustrates how to create an Invitation for Learning through a process of documentation: The educator has observed that many learners explore sounds through tapping objects, clanging loose parts, humming songs that are sung in large-group instruction, and stroking objects on uneven surfaces. Based on these observations, the educator has deduced that learners have a high level of musical interest. The educator has also witnessed some children making hurtful remarks about how one child is expressing their gender identity. Children have made comments such as "What boy wears pink?" and "Boys shouldn't have long hair!" They have asked this particular child, "What are you? A girl?" and "Why are you wearing that dress? Aren't you a boy?" The educator has reflected on the documentation gathered to determine how best to address the incidences of exclusion through musical and artistic expression. The educator's completed planning template (shown in figure 5.11) demonstrates how this documentation was used to inform an Invitation for Learning.

Playful Note

As you contemplate where you might offer Invitations for Learning within your space, think about learners' perspectives. Position yourself at their height; if possible, get on your knees. Experiencing your space through learners' eyes will give you much insight into how learning is marketed within your space.

Figure 5.9. Planning Invitations for Learning

Text	Image of Invitation for Learning

Conceptual Understanding/Big Idea

Curriculum Expectation(s)

Question

Materials	Organization of Materials
	(Parameters, Location)

Assess and Reflect
(Respond, Challenge, Extend)

Possible Next Steps

Figure 5.10. Considerations for Invitations for Learning

Considerations	What Do You Notice?
Positionality/proximity How are the materials positioned? Where have you positioned the parameters? How close are the materials to the learner?	
Organization (accessibility, material grouping, marketability) How have you organized the materials to highlight particular properties? What parameters have you established for play? How have you grouped the materials?	
Materials (diverse, texture, color, shape) How have you positioned the materials to maximize learning? How many materials have you offered? Are the materials open-ended? Do the materials reflect the various schemas observed by learners in play?	
Curriculum connections How do you make authentic connections to the curriculum or learning goals? Are multiple pathways available for accessing learning?	
Open-ended questions Is the question open-ended? What are the possibilities for play? How does the question provoke learners to think in various ways?	
Text How does the text support your learning goals? What ideas from the text align with the Invitation for Learning?	

Figure 5.11. Using Documentation to Inform an Invitation for Learning

Text
The educator has chosen the text *Red: A Crayon's Story* to respond to comments of exclusion that questioned a learner's gender expression. The book features a crayon who learns to love who they are.

Conceptual Understanding/Big Idea
The educator sees this learning goal as most responsive to the incidences of exclusion that have been documented.

Question
The question is open-ended and invites learners to uncover divergent ways of encouraging the character Red (e.g., learners can create a visual, write statements, or create song lyrics).

Materials
The open-materials allow learners to demonstrate their thinking in multiple ways that honor the one hundred languages.

Text	Image of Invitation for Learning

Conceptual Understanding/Big Idea
I am a member of a community. Some people in the community are the same as me, and some are different from me. All people are worthy of respect.

Curriculum Expectation(s)
Children will demonstrate an understanding of the diversity among individuals and families within schools and the wider community. They will communicate their thoughts, feelings, theories, and ideas through various art forms.

Question
How might you encourage Red?

Organization of Materials
(Parameters, Location)

Materials
- Colorful cubes → Vials of colorful water → Tiles
- Wood peg people → Seated table
- Mallet → Dry-erase markers → Small transparent bowls

Assess and Reflect
(Respond, Challenge, Extend)

Prompt using open-ended questions, anecdotal notes, videos, pictures, and noticing and naming.

Image of Invitation for Learning
Documenting what is offered through an image invites the educator to reflect on the learning experience and what revisions might need to be made.

Curriculum Expectation(s)
The learners' desire to express themselves artistically has provided an opportunity for the educator to draw on multiple expectations to address interests and meet learning needs.

Organization of Materials
The Invitation for Learning is offered on a seated table and includes clear containers that highlight the materials, along with tiles that provide a space for documentation.

Assess and Reflect
The educator will observe how learners respond to the invitation and ask questions to consider what changes need to be made to enrich or extend the learning.

Source: Curriculum expectations adapted from Ontario Ministry of Education (2016b).

Regifting Invitations for Learning

An Invitation for Learning is the gift that keeps on giving; thus, we must revise and reflect on this gift. As provocateurs, our role is to observe, assess, and rethink how invitations provoke children to reimagine the possibilities of play. Regifting the Invitation for Learning is an integral part of the learning cycle (see figure 5.12). As we move through this cycle, we deepen our intention.

Figure 5.12. The Learning Cycle

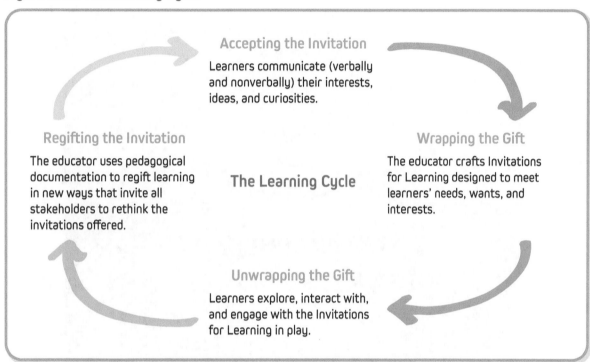

Accepting the Invitation
Learners communicate (verbally and nonverbally) their interests, ideas, and curiosities.

Wrapping the Gift
The educator crafts Invitations for Learning designed to meet learners' needs, wants, and interests.

The Learning Cycle

Regifting the Invitation
The educator uses pedagogical documentation to regift learning in new ways that invite all stakeholders to rethink the invitations offered.

Unwrapping the Gift
Learners explore, interact with, and engage with the Invitations for Learning in play.

Revitalizing Invitations for Learning serves several purposes:

→ To sustain and engage learners

→ To shift and broaden perspective

→ To respond to and validate learners' theories, curiosities, and wonders

→ To provoke and inquire

→ To introduce new ideas or conceptual understandings

→ To reestablish and extend learning goals

→ To market and highlight materials differently

→ To honor the "third teacher"

Invitations for Learning act as the "third teacher" in our learning spaces. As such, we must reflect on and revisit the ideas of time, space, relationships, and materials to create purposeful pivots for learners. You can regift an Invitation for Learning in multiple ways:

→ **Position the Invitation for Learning in a new area or at a different level in the learning space.** For example, an invitation on a table could be shifted to a large carpeted space, where learners can engage on the ground.

→ **Reposition materials, remove materials, or provide new open-ended materials to spark learners' interests.** Figure 5.13 shows how an educator has enabled new possibilities through a change in materials.

Figure 5.13. An Invitation for Learning Offered with Two Different Sets of Loose Parts

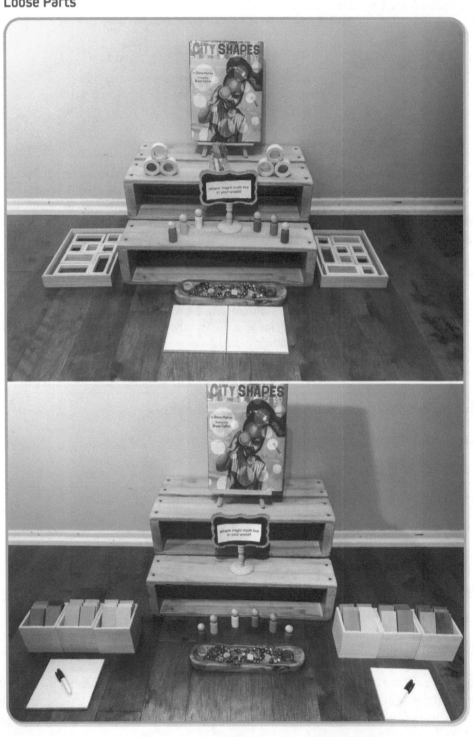

→ **Reframe the question to inspire new inquiry and provocation.** The section "Develop a Question" earlier in the chapter can help you consider how to craft a new question to elicit divergent thinking.

→ **Offer a new book, open a book to a particular point in the story, or shift to a new page to help deepen learners' understanding of the text, conceptual understanding, or learning goals.** Figure 5.14 shows an invitation set up to highlight a particular page in a book.

Figure 5.14. Highlighting a Specific Page of a Book in an Invitation for Learning

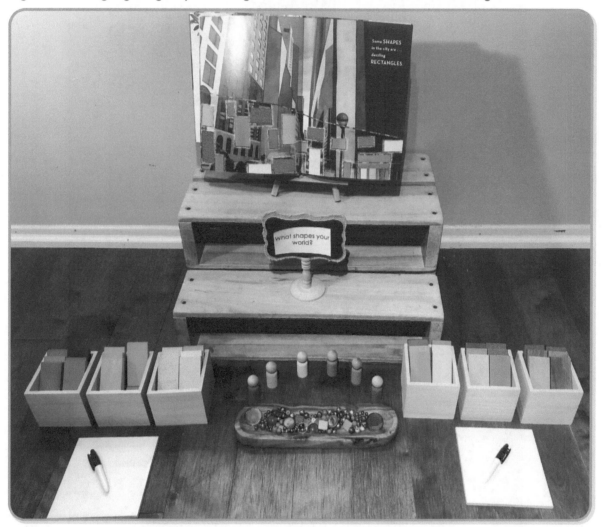

→ **Regift an Invitation for Learning at a later time to observe shifts and growth in children's learning.**

→ **Rescale what is offered in the Invitation for Learning, and engage in intentional scaffolding of the materials that are presented.** Figure 5.15 shows how an invitation has been transformed by offering fewer blocks to highlight particular properties and to support learners in their thinking and in using the materials more intentionally.

Figure 5.15. Rescaling and Scaffolding Materials

By rewrapping our gifts, we present learning in new ways through Invitations for Learning that are repurposed to bring about transformative experiences. As we reflect on our purpose in planning, we center the joys the gift will reveal.

→ **Change the parameter to invite a new perspective, or shift the means of documentation.** Figure 5.16 shows an Invitation for Learning using the book *Small World* by Ishta Mercurio. The educator added a mirror as a new medium for learners to document their ideas.

Figure 5.16. Adding a New Parameter (a Mirror) to an Invitation for Learning

Additional Considerations

Missed Invitations

As we purposely plan Invitations for Learning, it is important that we center learners' needs, interests, and identities. We may intentionally prepare learning opportunities we believe will respond to, challenge, and extend the concepts shared by children; however, at times, we are misguided in our pursuits. Being aware of these misconceptions will support us when we plan playful experiences.

Missed Invitation 1: Invitations for Learning should be created around a central theme.

Invitations for Learning offered in the learning environment should be responsive to what children do, say, or represent. When we follow children's interests, we need to ensure that the exploration of a big idea or concept is open-ended and does not restrict the thinking that may be provoked. Instead of focusing on a central theme, we think about grounding the Invitation for Learning in an inquiry question. For example, instead of offering an Invitation for Learning that focuses solely on skin tone (e.g., "What is your skin tone?"), the central question could be "What stories can we share about ourselves?"

We should move away from letting the *noun* (in this case, skin tone) drive learners' thinking. Theme-based Invitations for Learning are often limited in scope and speak only to opportunities for learners to remember and understand. By contrast, *verbs* (in this case, sharing stories about ourselves) invite learners to apply, evaluate, create, and analyze. Through this type of approach, we can provoke, investigate, explore, learn, and discover what children have to offer us. As we shared in chapter 3, our learning environments should not be created through a theme-based approach, and neither should our Invitations for Learning.

Missed Invitation 2: A book must be read to learners before it is offered within an Invitation for Learning.

Invitations for Learning can offer children books that have been read, unread, or read up to a particular point in class. The act of offering a text that children have not yet read is in itself a provocation because it allows you to see how learners approach the text; they may look at the illustrations, or they might use the materials to create based on their own predictions, perceptions, and interpretations of the story. These are learning skills and competencies that we want our children to develop. It is therefore unnecessary to read all books with learners before offering them within an Invitation for Learning.

Missed Invitation 3: All Invitations for Learning should accommodate the same number of learners.

We want our Invitations for Learning to be responsive to what we know about learners and the space in which we are offering this learning. Some offerings in spaces that are limited might be visited by two children, while others in larger spaces might invite more children. Parameters can guide how many learners choose to work in a particular space. We do, however, want to invite collaboration and communication among learners in various spaces, so we should not limit the number of children, even if it exceeds what the setup might have been designed for. In our own classroom experiences, learners themselves have become problem solvers when navigating their space. For example, we have observed a space where two learners interacted with an Invitation for Learning while a third child stood and manipulated the playful pieces offered.

If challenges arise, we can invite children to engage in conversation that allow them to problem-solve and strategize to find solutions that will best support the learning community. As inspiration, you can revisit "Our Playful Promise" from chapter 3.

Missed Invitation 4: All Invitations for Learning within the space should be changed at a fixed time.

As provocateurs, we must reflect on our documentation and use it to guide and support the shifts that we make over time to acknowledge learners' thoughts. When we wait until a fixed time to introduce, revitalize, or change Invitations for Learning, we deny opportunities for responsive action and new revelations of learning. As the learning evolves, new thoughts and ideas are revealed to us, and we leverage what we observe to foster a culture of thinking by introducing or revitalizing Invitations for Learning. However, learners can also guide us in identifying when we need to shelve a gift entirely or wait to regift it at a later time.

Missed Invitation 5: Questions must be read aloud to learners.

Inquiry-rich environments that invest in the belief that children are competent and capable will inspire questioning within the Invitations for Learning. Children may ask others to read the questions that are before them, or they may read the words they know and gather insight from the materials and the book. It is not essential that we enter into the practice of reading all questions aloud to learners. We value the importance of a print-rich environment that upholds the tenet of high expectations.

Missed Invitation 6: We should offer only one Invitation for Learning at a time in the learning space.

We encourage educators to plan and offer multiple Invitations for Learning that appeal to learners' one hundred languages. When we offer a limited number of invitations at a time (e.g., only two or three), this does not allow all learners to explore, create, or investigate to deepen their learning. If we do not provide multiple invitations, we may be creating conditions that foster tensions among learners who are limited by what has been offered.

Unraveling the Knots

Planning Invitations for Learning requires time, organization, an understanding of learners in the classroom, and responsiveness. We can create spaces that invite learning through play when we merge a child's interests, strengths, and needs with curriculum outcomes. As we embark on this journey for planning, we are reminded of the challenges that can present themselves.

Knot 1: Invitations for Learning should yield a specific product.

When offering Invitations for Learning, we focus on the process of thinking and what learners demonstrate over time. We invite you to reconsider one of the de-invitations from chapter 4, which is shown on the top of figure 5.17. In this setup, learners are expected to create a specific product based on the question and materials offered; by contrast, in the invitation shown on the bottom, children have multiple opportunities to share their thinking in varied ways.

Figure 5.17. A De-invitation versus an Invitation for Learning

We want you to consider how you may be tempted to use an invitation for the creation of a specific product and instead consider how an invitation should always allow for the various interpretations and ways of learning the children have. The results of an Invitation for Learning will never look the same across a group of children. We should celebrate differences in how learners use the materials instead of guiding them to create a specific product where all things look the same. Focus on the experience and exploration of materials as opposed to providing a sample or a finished product for learners to emulate.

Knot 2: Learners' engagement with Invitations for Learning fall on two opposite ends of the spectrum: some learners do not engage with Invitations for Learning at all, while others continuously visit a specific Invitation for Learning daily and rarely visit others when given the option to do so.

The livelihood of an Invitation for Learning relies on its ability to provoke and stimulate children's interests. If learners are not engaged in a particular invitation, we might gather children's ideas about that offering to support our planning. We encourage you to think about how you could revitalize the offering by revisiting the elements of an Invitation for Learning and the considerations to be used in designing it. You should also consider whether the learning conditions uphold or build the structure needed for rich play to thrive.

When we see learners revisiting an invitation frequently, this often reveals their interests. Children may be delivering the message that such experiences do not exist in other areas of the learning environment. Which of the one hundred languages is spoken within this invitation? Could this language exist in other Invitations for Learning offered in the environment? Consider how you might move materials, text, or similar questions into other learning spaces to entice children to take risks in their learning in alternative spaces.

Knot 3: All Invitations for Learning require revitalization.

While we want to revitalize learning opportunities to meet children's emerging needs and interests, not all invitations may yield these results. If much documentation has been gathered and a particular invitation's potential has been exhausted, then revitalization is not always necessary. In other words, children are not demonstrating new ideas connected to the learning goals or expectations, or their behavior patterns seem repetitive and similar outcomes are replicated. Additionally, the educator has utilized a number of strategies to revitalize the Invitation for Learning and the offering no longer draws the learners to play and engage. Remember that revitalization of invitations is meant to provoke or reinspire learners to imagine, explore, and create.

Pursuing the Gift

Planning is an important aspect of creating Invitations for Learning. We encourage you to think about what shifts you can make to encourage learning opportunities within your environment:

→ **Make a plan.** Use the guidelines included in this chapter to support you in creating your Invitations for Learning. Once you have offered an invitation in your space, capture a photo of it and add that image to your planning document. This will help you assess and reflect on your offerings.

→ **Let learners lead.** Develop Invitations for Learning that are responsive to what learners are interested in, or consider what you have observed based on children's interactions in relation to the learning goals and curriculum.

→ **Collaborate!** Plan with a colleague, teaching partner, or critical friend. Co-planning provides an opportunity for you to gain new perspectives and insight and can make the task of creating many Invitations for Learning more accessible.

Gifts of Learning

As we follow children's interests, theories, and thinking, we are led to wrap and unwrap the gift of thinking through Invitations for Learning. To summarize the key concepts explored in this chapter:

→ We need to leverage the gifts that children share through their strengths and interests in play.

→ We should move away from a culture of doing and instead cultivate a culture of thinking.

→ For Invitations for Learning, planning with purpose involves these key elements: following learners' interests; selecting a text, a photo, or an artifact, and connecting it to the curriculum; developing a question; considering the materials; organizing and marketing; and assessing and reflecting.

→ We need to revise Invitations for Learning to sustain engagement over time.

In this chapter, we have focused on the planning and organization of an Invitation for Learning. As you plan to offer Invitations for Learning in your environment, we challenge you to consider these questions:

→ How might children's interests, needs, and learning goals guide your planning pursuits?

→ What observations have you gathered to inform your planning?

→ How might you use the considerations for an Invitation for Learning to inform your planning?

Soon she had made a
whole *group* of really fun friends.

Friends that she could take with her
wherever she went.

Friends that wer...
easy to be...

How might you
connect to the
story?

Chapter 6
Playful Assessments

Invitations for Learning provide us with an opportunity to gather documentation, which can reveal learners' thinking. The book *Meesha Makes Friends* shares the experience of a young girl who has difficulty making friends. Meesha uses her creativity and artistic expression to design little toy friends that she carries with her. One day she meets someone new, who helps her learn that her interests and talents can help her make friends. The image shown here shares an Invitation for Learning connected to this book, with the question "How might you connect to the story?"

The images here and on pages 154–155 show how two children interacted with the Invitation for Learning connected to *Meesha Makes Friends*. The educator gathered the following documentation while observing these children:

Isla is tinkering with the materials as she considers how she will use the pieces to represent her ideas. She unravels a spool of ribbon, exposing its cardboard, which then becomes the head of her creation. Then she grabs two wood cylinders and bead necklaces and shares, "This is his mouth. This is a snowman!" She returns with a pink ribbon, which she wraps around the spool; she exclaims, "I created a snow girl that's Rapunzel!" while pointing to the long piece of ribbon she has added to her creation. "There's my snowman. He is a toy, and she loves it." She reveals that she has created a toy like the one the character makes in the story by saying, "That's a picture of her toy, just like the story."

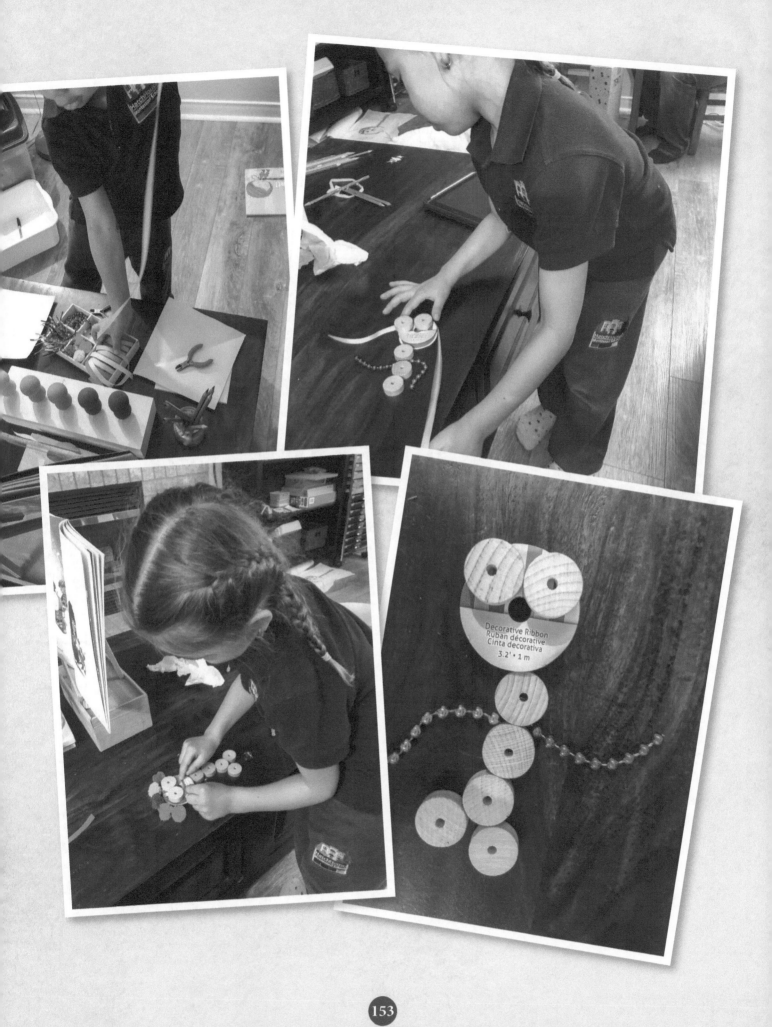

Ola says, "Me and Alyssa [a friend] are hiding behind the bean bag from the Roblox. Meesha was hiding behind the stairs. I was hiding from something, too." She uses scissors to cut the materials: "My favorite part of crafting is cutting." She cuts three pieces of ribbon and states, "This is small, medium, and big." She rearranges the materials from her story by scaling them according to size. As she finishes her creation, she looks at the educator nearby and shares, "I don't know what I would do if I didn't have any friends."

These learners had different experiences when engaged with the same Invitation for Learning. As you reflect on the documentation, ask yourself: *What have these children taught us from their experiences?*

What Moments Should We Capture?

A moment captured through documentation shares a story—one that is revealed through the invitation to play. We relish in the learning that has been experienced and invite the joy to live on through photos, videos, and more.

As children immerse themselves in learning through play, the diversity of their approaches and responses to the learning opportunities will yield a plethora of moments to capture. It can be daunting to determine exactly what to capture, along with how it can be captured to honor learners' thinking. As you embark on this exciting journey of offering play with intention in your spaces, you might ask this question: *What moments should I capture to inform my programming and next steps for learning?* We offer a few examples in figure 6.1.

Figure 6.1. Examples of Moments Captured in Documentation

Moment Captured	What Learners Have Said, Done, or Represented
Revelation	"Wow, look what we found!"
Curiosity	Learners use a magnifying glass to look at different angles of the specimen. "Look how the light shines over here. Why is it doing that?"
Achievement	"I finally did it!"
Application	Learners demonstrate skills learned from a large-group lesson in a variety of Invitations for Learning within the space.
Tension	"Why are you wearing this? It's dirty." "My mom says children should wear clean clothing."
Productive struggle	A child is creating a structure and tries to push a playful piece through a hole, but it just does not fit. "I'm trying to figure it out!"
Perseverance	A child notices that the pieces they are using to create are rolling off the parameters in different directions. After many attempts to find a solution, the child collects the pieces, places them on the surface at different angles, and demonstrates success.

The process of capturing a moment is negotiated between the documenter and the person being documented. The role of the educator is to document what children are saying, doing, and representing; as researchers, we uncover the truths revealed to us through play. Positioning ourselves as co-learners provides us with entry points for observation, as well as opportunities to reflect on the moments we have captured and to gain insights from learners about the thinking that has been made visible. We must ensure that our moments of documentation yield desirable outcomes for programming by considering these questions:

→ Will this moment support new learning for me?

→ Why should I document this moment, for this learner, at this time?

→ How can I capture the process of learning?

→ If I were to revisit the documentation at a later time, would it be sustainable and remain visible?

How Can We Capture the Moment?

Children's thinking can become visible in a variety of ways to serve the learners, families, and educators in the community. When creating a system to collect and gather documentation, we should employ various methods (Reimer et al. 2016):

→ Artifacts and representations (e.g., loose-part representations, visual representations, writing samples, dramatization)

→ Observational notes (e.g., input from learners, families, caregivers, or colleagues; personal anecdotal notes)

→ Digital recordings (e.g., videos, photographs, audio, social media sharing)

→ Student portfolios (e.g., digital portfolio, file folder portfolio)

→ Other records of learning (e.g., conferences, documentation panels, learning stories, interviews, surveys, running records)

Using more than one of these methods for documentation provides multiple opportunities for deeper reflection and perspective around learning. In reflecting on the types of documentation, consider these questions:

→ Which methods do you already rely heavily on?

→ Which methods have you not considered before now?

→ Which methods could give you more insight around learning?

→ How could you create a comprehensive collection of documentation that is varied?

What Is Pedagogical Documentation?

Documentation gathered from play gifts us with the evidence needed to assess learning and thinking. In play, we observe what children do, say, and represent to gain insights that guide us in developing next steps for programming. When we reflect on Isla and Ola from our earlier example, we see how the children's various languages are represented through the documentation.

Documentation becomes pedagogical when we have learned something new about a child. Carla Rinaldi (2001) invites us to think about pedagogical documentation as *visible listening*. When educators engage in this recursive form of dialogue with children, the cyclical process allows for growth in learning to be shared. The evidence collected becomes a living document that evolves and changes over time to reveal the progression of a child's learning. In addition, pedagogical documentation communicates key learning, growth in learning, and next steps (Ontario Ministry of Education 2016a).

The recursive nature of pedagogical documentation invites us to become reflective practitioners who position ourselves as co-learners. It offers us an opportunity to slow down our thinking, so that we can intentionally observe what children have done and use this information to plan purposefully. As children make thinking visible through their representations, ideas, and theories, we document the journey to communicate the shared understanding that has been attained. We use the evidence of learning that we capture over time to analyze and interpret information. Pedagogical documentation welcomes

→ partnerships in learning that strengthen relationships and honor multiple perspectives,

→ opportunities for educators to gather insights that inform next steps in teaching practice,

→ shared reflection and dialogue to make thinking visible for learners and educators,

→ every child's contributions and the rights of individual learners,

→ a child's growth in learning in relation to the learning goals and curriculum, and

→ each child's uniqueness in what they say, do, and represent.

The Process of Pedagogical Documentation

Our role as the educator is to observe learners as they interact with the learning environment, with other children, and with us. We collect information through documentation that captures children's work and makes their process of thinking visible. The process reveals insights that prompt us to shift instruction and programming to support children's growth in learning.

As learners interact with the space, with other children, and with us, we are constantly gathering evidence of learning that provides insights into children's thinking and learning. Think about a time when you noted the way a child reacted to a text and used that information to select another book for a read-aloud; in another instance, at the end of the day, you might have spoken to family members, who revealed a skill their child had developed at home, which helped you gain more insight into the child's strengths and interests. How do we take the knowledge gained in these moments and use it to benefit our program in a more intentional and systematic way so that assessment does not take on an additive approach? The cyclical process of pedagogical documentation (see figure 6.2) allows us to be responsive to learners by engaging in intentional observations, interpretations, and planning.

Figure 6.2. The Cyclical Process of Pedagogical Documentation

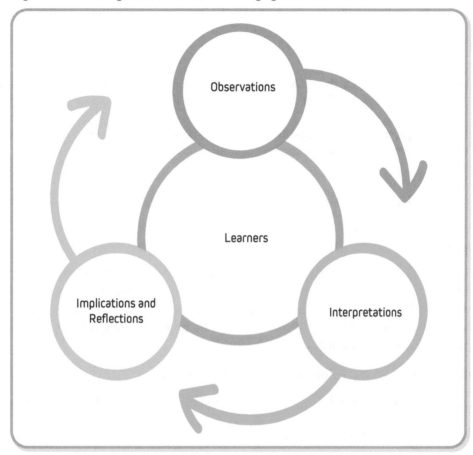

Source: Adapted from Ontario Ministry of Education (2015).

Observations

During this stage of the documentation process, we gather evidence by considering what we have observed. This stage can often be the most challenging for us as educators, as we tend to immediately interpret our observations. It is important to resist that temptation. As you gather documentation, you should carefully consider whether your observations capture the moment itself, as opposed to your thoughts or ideas about the moment. Figure 6.3 includes examples that illustrate the difference between observations and interpretations.

When our documentation neglects to capture the observations themselves, we might miss important information and impose interpretations that are actually misrepresentations of the story being captured. From whose perspective is the story being told? Remember, it's the child's story of learning that you're documenting.

In our own classroom experiences, there have been numerous occasions when we have entered spaces to see learners engaged in play and made interpretations of creations and shared them with the children, only to be told how inaccurate our interpretations were. We need to ensure that our observations are authentic to the experiences developed in the learning environment. You should collect documentation in a way that captures details that can provide insight that might not have been apparent during the experience. The process of thinking should be valued so that the documentation itself tells the story.

Figure 6.3. Observations versus Interpretations

Observations	Interpretations
Child A has placed a red block, then a blue block, then another red block on top of each other.	Child A is making a pattern as they create a tall tower.
Child C is moving wood peg people together and shares, "I'll huff, and I'll puff, and I'll blow you down."	Child C is retelling the story *The Three Little Pigs*.

Interpretations

As we review our documentation, we begin to consider what is revealed by the data. At this point, we should adopt an inquiry stance, where questioning becomes the approach. We take time to consider what we have captured and what this means as we notice and name the learning taking place. To organize your thinking and make sense of what you have documented, ask yourself the following questions:

→ What meaning can you gather from your observations?

→ How can you revisit your documentation with learners, their families, and other educators?

→ What are you now thinking?

→ What connections can you make to learning goals and the curriculum for yourself, for learners, and for their families?

We invite you to consider these questions as you review the pieces of information you have gathered and collected over time. This is the stage in documentation where you begin to learn something new about a child, which shifts your documentation to become *pedagogical documentation*.

Implications and Reflections

At this point in the process, we consider how to respond to our documentation, challenge learners, and extend their thinking and learning through our programming. We keep in mind the connections that we have made to the learning goals and curriculum as we make intentional decisions to provide a more responsive, holistic, and targeted approach to planning.

We consider the body of documentation we might have on a particular child or the larger group of children—the conversations they may have engaged in and other observations that help us determine pathways for new learning to emerge. As you reflect on and triangulate your documentation, these questions can guide your process and next steps:

→ How can pieces of documentation support your thinking?

→ What are the implications of this new information and learning?

→ What can you learn more about to support your growth in learning as a professional?

→ How can you share your reflections with learners, their families, and other educators?

Biases and Assumptions

As children unwrap the gifts of learning, they share untold stories with us. We sometimes impose our own thoughts and words on these stories, shifting the narratives that might have been. This serves to silence, reshape, and reinform the authentic narratives that once existed.

As an illustration of this idea, an educator observed a moment of play captured in figure 6.4, and the following interaction ensued:

> **Educator:** *"Wow! That is a magnificent ship you have created. Tell me more about it."*
>
> **Child:** *"This is not a ship. The lanterns are to send wishes to the ancestor. This is where the ancestors are [pointing at the wood peg people in the center of the creation]. The people go here, and smoke comes, and they speak to their ancestors."*
>
> *The child also shares that she has observed lanterns being released during her travels to Asia.*

Figure 6.4. A Moment in Play Misinterpreted by the Educator

This interaction leads us to ask:

→ How many times have we silenced or influenced children's voices based on our own interpretations of their work?

→ How do our positions of power and privilege shape, influence, and drive learners to engage in performative and submissive interactions? How does this serve to appease us as educators, as opposed to truly honoring the stories that live within these moments?

→ How do our subjectivities cloud our judgment when documenting children's learning?

Some children may be susceptible to the educator's interpretations and may validate or confirm the educator's thoughts and ideas to please the educator. When we probe for understanding and question too much, children's thoughts become conflated with our own, and we move further away from the real meaning of the moment.

> The choices educators make about *what* to document reveal their values and what they deem important to notice about children. As educators document children's learning, they must be aware of their own subjectivity and biases—that is, they must recognize that they are capturing and representing children's learning through the lens of their particular perspective on children and on how children learn. (Ontario Ministry of Education 2016b, 38)

There is value in interpreting documentation; however, we must be cognizant of the biases we hold and how they influence our interpretations. Through the process of documentation, we learn more about children's families and communities. We gain perspective of learners' cultural beliefs, values, and traditions, and we need to ensure that our methods of documentation honor these practices and beliefs. Here are a few examples of when families have guided our documentation practices:

→ Some families do not want photos taken of their children, due to a mistrust in the educational system. For other families, capturing photos of learners would contradict their spiritual beliefs.

→ Some families honor oral storytelling and traditions and see more value and engagement in this form of documentation than they do for written forms of communication.

→ Some families need documentation to be shared in a more accessible form (e.g., audio, translations, Braille).

→ Families with learners who have more than one living space may request ongoing communication to be shared simultaneously.

When we listen to the voices of learners, families, and communities, we can adopt more responsive methods for collecting and sharing documentation and bridge communication in various spaces for learning. We must be reflective practitioners by considering the biases and assumptions we hold when we engage in the process of documentation. You can do this by asking yourself the following questions:

Observations

→ Whose work are you documenting? What are the identities of these learners?

→ Whose work have you not highlighted through documentation?

→ What methods are you using for documentation? Do your methods capture learners' strengths? (For example, you may be continually asking learners to demonstrate their thinking in written form, when they prefer to express themselves in other ways.)

→ Are you excessively documenting the work of learners with particular identities? If so, why might you be doing this?

→ How have you partnered with families to collect documentation?

Interpretations

→ What documentation are you relying on to support your thinking?

→ What aspects of the curriculum or learning goals are overly represented in your interpretations? Which are underrepresented?

Implications and Reflections

→ How might your preconceived notions of children and their capabilities influence your next steps?

→ Who are you sharing your reflections with? While sharing reflections, who might you be missing and why?

→ How are learners' voices honored through your process of reflection?

Reducing Bias in Assessments

Our biases and assumptions in assessment impact how we gather, interpret, and reflect on documentation. We recognize that we can never fully eliminate biases within our assessment practices; however, we can strive to engage in actions that reduce biases. These strategies can help you in your journey:

1. **Engage in self-reflection.**

   When we position ourselves as co-learners, we must acknowledge our shifting roles as educators, researchers, and learners. Sometimes, we may occupy all three roles at once. Through this approach, we invite ourselves to engage in reflection. We locate our social identities, we recognize our power and privilege as educators, and we consider where our assumptions and biases are rooted. Being self-aware requires ongoing learning, unlearning, and relearning anew.

2. **Use multiple forms of documentation to capture thinking and learning.**

   Keep in mind the guidelines we shared earlier in the chapter about capturing the moment, so that you can gather and collect documentation that is varied and diverse. Your collection of documentation should provide a comprehensive perspective of children's work and demonstrate a range of samples. There is a danger in capturing documentation from a singular source, as it provides us with limited information about a child's thinking. We may consider gathering photos, videos, anecdotal notes, and other modes of documentation, from multiple contexts, of a child to then broaden our understanding of their strengths and needs.

3. **Use an inquiry stance to analyze documentation.**

   The process of documentation invites us to be curious about what children are saying, doing, and representing. Throughout this process, it's important to adopt an inquiry stance as you question your way to new theories, ideas, and understanding of learners and their growth in learning. Reconsider what you once knew. What we ask of our learners as inquirers should also be asked of ourselves as educators.

4. **Partner with learners, families, colleagues, and the community.**

   Collaboration is a significant part of the documentation process. We gain a holistic interpretation of children and their thinking when we invite learners, educators, families, and community members to join us as we learn together. Engaging in collaborative and reflective dialogue with individuals who provide alternative perspectives deepens our understanding of children.

If we are not careful, our biases may influence our interpretations of the documentation. We have a responsibility to uphold what children share with us in their playful pursuits. We run the risk of denying voices and infringing upon the thoughts and ideas that are shared. Our biases may limit the scope for interpretation, which filters the possibilities for learning.

Stages of Pedagogical Documentation

The process of pedagogical documentation is twofold in that we make children's thinking and learning visible while reflecting on our own preconceptions. In *THINQ Kindergarten: Inquiry-Based Learning in the Kindergarten Classroom* (2016), Joan Reimer and her colleagues outline characteristic stages of documentation that can guide our thinking for intentional planning and self-assessment. In figure 6.5, we consider those stages and what they might mean in the context of a play-based learning environment. The stages and defining characteristics support educators in making choices that provide more of a comprehensive view of themselves as documenters and those they document. We share the stages with you as a reference point for your own journey and thinking related to documentation.

Figure 6.5. Characteristic Stages of Documentation

Stages of Documentation	Characteristics
Choosing to document	The educator may be unsure of what to capture in play (e.g., photos of loose-parts creations, videos of children playing collaboratively together).
	The educator collects various creations in play with limited intention.
	The educator is the sole collector of the documentation, without consulting the protagonists.
	There is an emphasis on the end product created in play.
Exploring ways to collect and share documentation	The educator begins to invite the protagonists to view the documentation they've collected (e.g., sending photos in a family newsletter).
	There is evidence of documentation shared in the learning environment.
	The educator begins to take risks in exploring new ways to document (e.g., using a voice-recording app).
	The educator still controls what is collected and shared with children and families (e.g., by creating slideshows of children's creations).
Focusing on capturing thinking and learning	The educator is more intentional in determining which learning to capture.
	The educator centers documentation on the process of learning, rather than the finished product in play.
	Learners are invited to choose the documentation they would like to share from their playful experiences.
	Time is dedicated within the flow of the day (see chapter 2) for children to share and reflect.
Making thinking and learning visible	The educator uses various forms of documentation to share the journey of children's learning.
	Learners are invited to conference with the educator, and evidence of their voice is revealed within the documentation story that is shared.
	The documentation begins to tell a story that builds over time. Through captions and comments, context is given for how the learning has emerged.
	Children and educators begin to notice and name learning connected to the curriculum and the program.
	The educator may highlight curriculum expectations demonstrated in play (e.g., "Rizwan has created a tower with repeating patterns that is also symmetrical").
Being responsive and planning next steps in learning	The educator reviews and reflects on the documentation process to determine next steps in programming; they may also do this in collaboration with the protagonists.
	The educator regularly conferences with learners to set goals and extend learning.
	The educator identifies professional learning needs and drafts plans to further their own learning.

Source: Adapted from Reimer et al. (2016).

Reflecting on these stages allows us to slow down our observations and our intentions in capturing learning to make children's stories visible. The stages are intended to support our own documentation, and we may see ourselves reflected in various stages over time. Our current stage may depend on the subject matter, learners, the learning goals, shifts in the learning environment, or a lack of time, to name a few factors. No matter where we are in the process, we need to center learners in authentic and meaningful ways.

→ Which characteristics in figure 6.5 align with your current practice?

→ How can the stages of the process inform your next steps for documentation?

→ How can you center student thinking and learning within your documentation?

Honoring Student Voices in Documentation

In her autobiography, Zora Neale Hurston wrote, "There is no greater agony than bearing an untold story inside you" (1942, 213). Hurston's statement reminds us of the power that is held within the role of the documenter. Think about the stories that are shared in the learning environment. Who is telling the story, whose lens is capturing its authenticity, and what is missing? We reveal learners' potential when we believe in their capabilities and provide them with tools to share their stories from their own perspectives.

Take a look at the loose-parts creation captured in figure 6.6, and ask yourself these questions:

→ What do you see, think, and wonder about this creation?

→ What does this creation tell us about the child's thinking?

→ Is this enough information to reveal learning?

→ Have we gathered enough data to best support this learner?

Figure 6.6. A Child's Loose-Part Creation

If we pay attention to the answers to these questions, they will lead us to transform our practice in ways that honor and center children. We are reminded that what our learners offer back to us is a gift. Paying close attention to these gifts requires us to look closely at the process. We now build on the photo shared in figure 6.6 to fully explore this child's story.

Sharing a Child's Story

For this playful experience, the child was invited to engage with the question "What might you create?" As the educator observed the child engaging in this playful experience, so much learning happened beyond what was asked of the child. The educator was able to capture multiple steps within this process. In figure 6.7, we see the process of a child's thinking made visible. The child initially sorted the materials by color and said, "I am going to build a castle." He was observed joining blocks together to create structures. Once the structures were complete, he created an enclosure around them; he then pointed to his creation and stated, "This is my kingdom." He immediately began storytelling and shared more details about his structure: "My castle is for queens and kings. There's a dragon trying to destroy the castle. The knight will fight the dragons!" The child then chose cubes to use to measure the perimeter of the structure, but after realizing that he didn't have enough cubes to go all the way around, he switched to sticks.

Figure 6.7. The Process of a Child's Thinking Made Visible

This learner used the materials in creative ways. The educator did not notice the dragon that the child had mentioned in the story until the educator asked the child which perspective he wanted his work to be documented from; the child suggested an aerial view (see figure 6.8). When documenting learners' creations, it is important that we ask children how they would like their work to be captured. Had the educator in this scenario not done this, we would have missed the aerial view that revealed the dragon in the child's oral story.

Figure 6.8. The Dragon Revealed

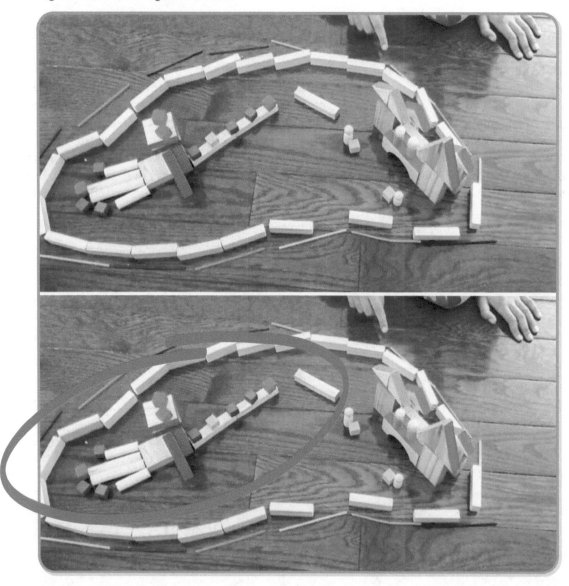

As we saw in the previously described experience, lots of learning occurred that could have been missed if the educator had captured only the product and had not documented the process. As we gather documentation of learners in play, we must remember that the journey is as enriching as the destination. The journey might take us down divergent pathways of understanding, so we need to highlight what it presents to us.

As children interact with Invitations for Learning, you can honor the process of their thinking and learning through these strategies, which we explore next:

→ Self-documentation

→ Responding to, challenging, and extending thinking

→ Noticing and naming the learning

→ Conferencing

Self-Documentation

Empowering learners to document their own journey enables them to lead the learning and control their narratives and perspectives in play. In earlier chapters, we considered the importance of the protagonist and their role; this partnership creates opportunities for deeper engagement. When we maintain high expectations for learners and provide them with tools to document their own work, they can capture astounding things that support the documentation process. At the most basic level, we must understand that, realistically, we cannot capture the process of all children in play at all times throughout the day. Partnering with learners and promoting self-documentation will help you capture more experiences and gather more insight into children's work. As learners contribute to the process of documentation, keep in mind that they also move through the stages previously outlined in figure 6.8. Explicit instruction and modeling are required for children to effectively capture their thinking and learning. You may want to share examples and non-examples to help children effectively capture what they say, do, and represent in play. You can use these strategies to encourage self-documentation in your learning environment:

→ Offer a variety of documentation tools (e.g., paper, writing utensils, cameras, small clipboards, tablets) within your space that are accessible to children at all times.

→ Model how to use various child-friendly apps (e.g., SeeSaw) and documentation tools.

→ Co-construct expectations with learners around ways to self-document.

→ Conduct mini-lessons on effective ways to capture a photo or video.

→ Praise and prompt learners when they initiate documentation.

→ Harness the skills of proficient documenters in the learning community to support their peers.

Providing opportunities for children to self-document requires establishing routines, being consistent, and patience. We encourage you to take the risk and release responsibility for your learners to assume the roles of documenters. When children begin to document, they become more reflective of what they capture, and their documentation may become more aligned with the learning goals. In addition, educators are relieved of the responsibility of documenting every moment of learning.

Responding to, Challenging, and Extending Thinking

When playful experiences offer multiple entry points for learners, the documentation we gather will also reveal multiple curriculum connections. To revisit our earlier example (see figures 6.8– 6.10), offering a measurement worksheet to the child who created the kingdom probably would not have yielded such rich documentation. As we gather evidence of learning, we must consider how we might respond to, challenge, and extend playful experiences to gain more information. Consider how your wonderings could be used to provoke further thought for children, as well as how your documentation could lend itself to further planning of playful learning experiences or direct instruction.

From documenting the process of a child building a kingdom, the educator was able to gather information about the learner's ability to create a story that connected to his creation. He demonstrated his understanding of measuring perimeter by selecting nonstandard units for measurement. The educator also noted a misconception: as the child used sticks for measuring, he was observed overlapping the sticks in some areas and leaving gaps in others. This learning moment inspired the educator to intentionally select a text for a different playful experience that would further explore the concept of measurement (see figure 6.9). This Invitation for Learning highlighted the book *Boxitects* by Kim Smith, which tells the story of a young girl who designs and innovates using boxes. She is paired with a partner who challengers her to create tall structures using boxes and has to learn how to collaborate and problem-solve. In this invitation, the educator posed the question "What might you design?" and paired the book with blocks, scouring pads, ribbons, paper clips, wood cubes, peg people, wood sticks, tiles, and dry-erase markers.

Through this Invitation for Learning, the educator aimed to fuel learners' interest in building while also providing entry points for measurement and other learning opportunities. As learners interacted with this offering, the educator closely monitored and observed how children used the playful pieces to determine next steps for large-group and small-group instruction.

Figure 6.9. An Invitation for Learning Inspired by Documentation

The gifts that we wrap and offer to our learners invite them to share their ideas and wonders in divergent ways. Invitations for Learning provide ideal opportunities to *respond to*, *challenge*, and *extend* learners' thinking. As you consider your next moves to maximize growth and learning in your space, you can use these strategies to shift your pedagogical approaches:

Respond:

→ Probe and ask open-ended questions.

→ Enter learners' play to invite new thinking.

→ Gather resources, artifacts, and photos that respond to learners' strengths, interests, and needs.

→ Connect with families and community members.

Challenge:

→ Use documentation to leverage more thinking and questions in large-group and small-group settings.

→ Layer in new materials.

→ Continue to probe and ask open-ended questions.

→ Continue to enter learners' play to challenge new ways of thinking (e.g., parallel play with learners).

→ Open up dialogue to the larger group by asking them to problem-solve collaboratively.

→ Assess your offerings through documentation to support the process of revitalizing Invitations for Learning.

Extend:

→ Layer in additional learning opportunities (e.g., provocations or Invitations for Learning that align with children's thinking).

→ Offer explicit instruction to address learners' needs in a large-group or small-group setting.

→ Invite families and community members to broaden understanding connected to the learning experiences.

→ Gather more information and research to expand your professional repertoire.

Noticing and Naming the Learning

As educators, we must remember to position ourselves as co-learners first when children share their learning through documentation. In whole-group experiences, we invite children to notice and name their learning as they tap into their metacognitive processes—that is, as they think about their own thinking. The following strategies support the process of noticing and naming:

→ Share specific documentation of children's work in play (e.g., a photo, an audio recording, a short video clip, an artifact), and provide space for learners to notice and name their thinking. Consider how the documentation you have gathered will help deepen the learning experience. You can revisit the section "What Moments Should We Capture?" earlier in the chapter to determine how you can harness the documentation necessary to provoke thinking.

→ Invite children to respond to one another's work. This presents an opportunity to honor their perspectives and ideas as they notice and name, ask questions, and challenge their peers in new ways.

→ Ask questions, probe, and make connections to the learning goals that emerge from the conversation.

You can sustain learning and inspire emerging interests and knowledge by creating structures within the flow of the day (see chapter 2) that allow for consolidation of playful experiences. We suggest that this be done in a large-group context, but we invite you to consider how you can offer moments for children to notice and name in small-group experiences as well.

Conferencing

Through conferencing, educators can create spaces that build trust and foster intimate moments where children can share meaningful learning and information. In small groups or one on one, educators may meet with children to discuss documentation that was collected; they may gather evidence to support previous conversations with learners, ask questions to gain more clarity, or have children reflect on learning goals. As we confer with learners, we propel them toward their next steps and guide them in determining how they can navigate materials and the physical learning space in new ways over time. Develop systems and routines for conferencing with children. Approaching this process in a systematic way will help you better anticipate who needs to be seen and who has been missed. The strategies that we recommend for conferencing are responsive to each child and will vary based on time, space, materials, and relationships. Here are strategic actions you can take:

> **Playful Note**
>
> Remember that families and the community serve as resources that can expand children's thinking. You can share documented moments of play with families and invite them to respond to, challenge, and extend learners' thinking. This can bridge communication and allow families and communities an opportunity to inform programming from an alternative perspective. Consider using apps that support continual dialogue between educators, families, and community members.

- → Revisit documentation with learners, which will allow you to gain further insight into what they might have been saying, doing, or representing while in play.

- → Ask children open-ended questions. Remember that what you ask and how you ask it might reveal your own biases and interpretations. As a co-learner in this process, you should ask questions that provide a platform for learners to share their ideas, processes, and thinking.

- → Provide focused instruction to ensure learning needs are met based on what the documentation has revealed.

Conferencing targets the strengths and needs of learners. We recommend dedicating time for small group or individual meetings that build upon the insights and learning of children. You can use the valuable information you gather to inform your next instructional moves.

Sharing and Celebrating Learning

Children are protagonists who inspire other learners through their playful work. The purpose of sharing documentation with children, their families, and other educators is to provoke, celebrate, and promote learning. There are many ways for us to highlight what children have revealed in play. When you share and celebrate learning through documentation, provide opportunities for children to observe and respond to what is offered. This might take the form of displaying documentation within the learning space, or it might happen through noticing and naming during designated times within the flow of the day.

Learners may revisit documentation displayed in the learning environment during play. A child may look back at a photo of a tower they have constructed and share their visions and ideas for how they will rebuild and redesign this structure to be taller and sturdier. Sharing documentation within your space goes beyond appealing simply to aesthetics. We encourage you to consider how you can make learning visible in ways that serve children, push their thinking, and provide a resource that can be revisited as it evolves and grows over time. When you display learners' contributions and moments of learning in a celebratory way, learners may be inspired to revisit and reinvest in a particular moment to demonstrate new knowledge. They may also invite other children to interact, share, and build on the experience. You can consider sharing and celebrating learners' work in these ways:

- → Documentation panels

- → Community events and displays

- → Gallery moves*

- → Sharing and reflection times within the flow of the day

- → Family conferences

- → Communication to families in the learning community

- → Blogs and websites

When we share and celebrate learners' work in these ways, we continue to foster a sense of belonging and contributing for children in the space. Establishing these practices in our learning environment serves to center and amplify learners' actions, words, and deeds. Documentation is an ongoing process that grows, evolves, and changes as a living body of work. This process is a communal one that involves all protagonists. "To feel a sense of belonging, to be part of a larger endeavor, to share meanings—these are rights of everyone involved in the educational process, whether teachers, children, or parents" (Rinaldi 1998, 114).

*Note that the term *gallery move* disrupts notions or concepts about ability, bodies, and movement. The use of the term *gallery walk* excludes learners who access movement in a variety of ways. As we discussed in previous chapters, we should consider how the words used in the classroom affect learners.

Additional Considerations

Missed Invitations

Children provide us with great insight into their thinking and learning when we take the time to slow down and observe. Pedagogical documentation offers us a window that invites us as educators to respond to, challenge, and extend thinking. In this process, we may sometimes miss the opportunities that invite us to pedagogically pivot and go deeper in learning.

Missed Invitation 1: Only the final product should be captured for assessment.

Educators sometimes condition children to think that their learning and creations in play should be captured only once they are finished. We need to move away from memorializing moments that highlight only the end product. We should instead document moments of learning that capture a learner's thoughts throughout the process of play. This approach leads us to learn more, as it is comprehensive and holistically representative of learners' thinking over time.

Missed Invitation 2: Documentation can be used to create a beautiful learning environment.

The documentation that surrounds the learning environment should reveal the journey in learning that unfolds over time. Although it is important to create an inviting space, the documentation that we share should also serve the purpose of provoking continuous learning in the space. It serves as a living document that shifts to reveal new things that inform and reinform the audience, whether it consists of learners, educators, or families. The evidence of learning that we share should be accessible to the audience and invite new perspectives. As educators, we can model how documentation informs learning by using it as an instructional tool to support inquiry-based learning. For example, in the middle of large-group instruction, the educator may revisit documentation of a strategy revealed by a child in another learning experience to support the current instructional focus. When deciding how to display pedagogical documentation in your space, ask yourself these questions:

→ Who will the documentation inspire or impact within the learning environment?

→ Where will the documentation be positioned? Will the location of the documentation be accessible to learners? How can children contribute to this process?

→ Why is this documentation being shared in the learning environment? How can it be used to inspire, affirm, and inform learners' thinking?

→ How can you leverage documentation as an instructional tool?

→ When does the documentation no longer support the learning?

Missed Invitation 3: Authentic assessment cannot be gathered through play-based learning.

As discussed in previous chapters, we see play as the vehicle for learning. When we intentionally craft open-ended experiences through Invitations for Learning, we tap into the capacity to access more information that supports our assessment practices. This allows us to pivot pedagogically and provide intentional support through instruction and play experiences that respond to, extend, and challenge thinking. As Albert Einstein once said, "play is the highest form of research." There is much that can be learned from children in play.

Unraveling the Knots

The gifts of pedagogical documentation are the revelations of learning that center a child's thoughts. At times, we may extract meaningful moments that share children's interests, curiosities, identities, and needs; however, there are moments within this process that may stray from learners' authentic interpretations. We invite you to consider the knots that entangle the process of pedagogical documentation along the way.

Knot 1: How do you honor documentation while meeting district standards?

As educators, we must know our curriculum and the learning goals that connect to the expectations outlined for achievement. Purposefully revisiting our documentation and making explicit connections to curriculum during our planning helps ensure that we are meeting district standards.

Knot 2: Whose ideas are shared and honored within documentation? And from whose perspective?

We must always center learners' voices in the process of capturing, interpreting, and responding to documentation. Longstanding legacies that position the educator as the sole holder of assessment, learning, and thinking perpetuate the power dynamic that has been interwoven into the fabric of education. How often do you hear families share that they are shocked by what is conveyed about their children through documentation, as it has not been part of the conversation with all protagonists? We encourage you to consider the strategic actions outlined in this chapter as ways to center learners' voices and dismantle power structures established through assessment processes.

Knot 3: Educators feel the need to quickly support learners when they are approaching challenges.

At times, educators intercede too quickly in play. This does not always allow for productive struggle to unfold in ways that help children better problem-solve and innovate. Learning is a process that does not always immediately provide the answer. Time and intentional moves in teaching will support the learning. Learners may also approach the educator with their questions and challenges during play. For example, a learner may say, "I cannot get the tower to stand tall. Why isn't it working for me?" Instead of immediately providing answers, we should:

Observe and listen to children because when they ask "why?" they are not simply asking for the answer from you. They are requesting the courage to find a collection of possible answers. This attitude of the child means that the child is a real researcher. As human beings, we are all researchers of the meaning of life. (Rinaldi 2001, 4)

Knot 4: Children mimic the conditions you have established for documentation.

Children may reveal how they have become conditioned to your documentation habits. For example, children may start to approach you when they are done representing their ideas and say, "You can take my picture now." Or you might insist that a child write or draw a picture of their creation in play before moving to another learning opportunity. While we want to establish conditions and protocols for documentation, we must reflect on our practices and whether we rely on a particular form of documentation. We should also be cognizant of the power dynamics that we may be creating when we enforce such expectations within play. We invite you to center flexibility and harness children's potential in the process of pedagogical documentation.

Pursuing the Gift

Now that you have gained more understanding of pedagogical documentation, you can take these small shifts to support your programming:

→ **Start with what you know.** Capture learning in play using tools that are familiar to you (e.g., capture photos or videos with a tablet, or offer clipboards and writing tools within your space that learners can draw or write with). Once your space offers tools for documentation, it will support the collection of learning that is needed for analysis.

→ **Create a plan.** As you embark on your documentation journey, it is important to establish some routines. It is helpful to select a small group of learners you can observe at different times of the day to gather more information. As you develop your plan, consider strategies that can support you in collecting what learners say, do, or represent. For example, if you notice that an Invitation for Learning has piqued the interest of a group of learners, this area may become a focal point for your documentation. Or you might consider looking at a group of learners and selecting a few children you are most curious about. Make a plan and set goals that are reasonable for you and sustainable over time.

→ **Make time to review and reflect.** Documentation becomes pedagogical when we learn something new about children; thus, we must set aside time to review what we have collected. Consider meeting regularly with a teaching partner or colleague, building in time at the end of the day to review and analyze what you have gathered.

Gifts of Learning

At this point in our journey, we have uncovered the power of pedagogical documentation and how it enriches playful programming. To summarize the key concepts explored in this chapter:

→ Documenting children's engagement with an Invitation for Learning can reveal their divergent thinking.

→ We should aim to capture moments that make thinking visible.

→ We can use a variety of methods to capture moments that reveal authentic and meaningful learning.

→ Documentation becomes pedagogical when we have learned something new about a child.

→ The cyclical process of documentation involves observing, interpreting, and reflecting.

→ We need to be mindful of how our biases can influence our documentation.

→ We can take strategic actions to reduce bias in our assessments.

→ There are multiple stages of documentation; throughout the process, we need to honor and center children's voices.

→ We can honor children's thinking and learning through self-documentation; by responding to, challenging, and extending thinking; by noticing and naming the learning; and through conferencing.

→ Our documentation can help share and celebrate children's contributions and learning over time.

This chapter has celebrated how the process of documentation unfolds to center children's ideas. As you move through the stages of pedagogical documentation, we encourage you to be mindful of the following questions:

→ How might the playful learning opportunities offered in your space yield multiple outcomes for learning that can be documented?

→ How might various sources of documentation reveal learning and support your process for planning?

→ How might you honor the process of pedagogical documentation in your practice?

Where am I from?

YAMILE

Abuelo thinks.
His eyes squint, like he's looking
inside his heart for an answer.

Where are you from?

My Learning

Chapter 7
Playful Partnerships

It's a busy morning in an early years classroom; a book has just been read, and children have transitioned into exploration time. As they move throughout the learning environment, interacting with the Invitations for Learning that are offered, Avery has just arrived with their mom, and they are busy working together to get Avery's coat and backpack hung. Ms. Ali quickly turns to her teaching partner, Mrs. Beena, and asks, "Can you deal with them? You know you're better with that mom."

Mrs. Beena approaches the family and warmly greets them.

"Sorry we're late again. There was so much going on this morning that we missed our bus," Avery's mom shares as she moves quickly to give Avery a goodbye kiss.

Mrs. Beena extends a hand to Avery and says, "I am just so glad Avery is here now. They missed the morning story, but I'm going to find some time to share it with them today. I think they will really like it."

Avery's mom replies, "Oh, okay. You probably could do it now. It looks like they are just playing anyway," then quickly exits.

Ms. Ali comes over to Mrs. Beena, shaking her head with disapproval. "I wish Mom would get it together. We had the very same problem with the older sibling when they were in this class. I'm glad you are able to communicate with her better than I can."

> The culture you develop sets the tone, reflects who you are, and expresses how you want to live and learn with children. If you strive for joyful days and see yourself as a learner right alongside children and their families, you'll work with a set of values, not just regulation. (Curtis and Carter 2017, 29)

The relationships that we build with families begin with the values and disposition that we establish within our learning community. As you consider the scenario of Avery's arrival at school, think about this question: *What values are being expressed by the educators and by the family?*

We offer this scenario to consider some of the multiple perspectives and misinterpretations that might exist when partnering with families.

→ While Ms. Ali has acknowledged that Mrs. Beena has a better relationship with Avery's family, she doesn't take the initiative to engage with Avery's mother in this moment. Sometimes, educators fail to foster relationships with families, relying on other colleagues to be the conduit of communication.

→ Mrs. Beena's flexibility and responsiveness to the interests and needs of the child fosters a welcoming and caring space that honors partnerships with families. Ms. Ali's perceptions of the family are rooted in previous experiences. The biases we may hold about learners and their families shape the way interactions may occur.

→ Avery's mother shared how she values play when she directed Mrs. Beena to read a story instead of supporting Avery's transition to exploration time. When offering a play-based environment, families can hold misconceptions about play and its importance. This may create tensions that hinder and shape the course of dialogue for learning.

Placing learners at the center supports creating better lines of communication and fosters stronger ties and greater understanding of one another.

Our Views of Families

As educators, we have the honor of partnering with families who entrust us with their children. Our beliefs, attitudes, and perspectives toward families influence our programs and practices. We center children in all that we do and take into consideration each protagonist who supports a child's growth and learning. The diagram in figure 7.1 illustrates variables that may affect children's development on their learning trajectory. Families are diverse, hold multiple perspectives, and provide us with funds of knowledge that make valuable contributions to learning. As we shift our mindsets and adapt a co-learning stance in partnership with children and families, we can learn much from the families and communities we work with.

Our goal is to create positive relationships that center learners and respond to families with a sense of care. We are champions for the same cause: the growth and success of children.

> As families begin to trust that you care about and believe in their child, they will be more willing to open up to you about their hopes, beliefs, and concerns. Families that feel accepted and respected are also far more open to listening to you when you talk about what they are doing in the classroom and why you are doing it. (Derman-Sparks 2020, 64)

Figure 7.1. Factors in a Child's Learning Trajectory

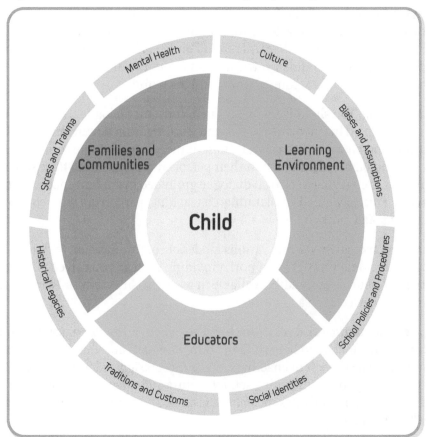

Key Characteristics of Family Partnerships

We should view learners' families as competent contributors whose expertise can help us enrich learning experiences. Partnering with families supports learners in all developmental domains (cognitive, social, emotional, and physical). Children who observe positive interactions between their families and educators learn to develop ways to create positive and trusting relationships with others. "Children's academic growth benefits from instructional coherence (when the learning in the program is supported by the learning at home and vice-versa)" (Massachusetts Department of Early Education and Care and WGBH Educational Foundation n.d., para. 17). Families and educators who are invested in learning from each other develop a shared understanding of children's learning goals and needs and the ways in which play-based programming can support these needs.

Leveraging partnerships is vitally important for supporting children's growth in learning. Learning should not happen without the contribution and collaboration of protagonists who together create a common language that merges shared goals, visions, and aspirations.

You can use these strategies to help foster family partnerships:

→ **Establish connections.** Fostering initial connections allows families to gain insight into who you are through open dialogue and communication. As an educator, you should aim to support and build rapport with learners and families. The materials and resources offered in your space of learning should be intricately and intentionally woven to affirm, inspire, and celebrate multiple families, communities, and the world.

→ **Center learning.** You should aim to engage in constant dialogue that centers children and their learning. This involves sharing and learning from documentation collected at school and at home, as well as a shift from servitude to sustainable solidarity. In other words, you should help families shift their perspective from seeing themselves serving only as volunteers to engaging in critical dialogue grounded in student success and learning approaches. This may entail co-planning, co-teaching, partnering with community organizations, and more.

→ **Advocate for access.** By valuing various modes of communication (e.g., honoring home languages, providing translator support, providing videos), you can ensure that necessary support and resources are readily available in ways that are seamlessly integrated into the program (not viewed as an add-on).

→ **Shift power dynamics and relationships.** You should provide space for families to share their competencies to help shift and transform decision-making for educational programming. The process of enacting change must be ignited by the visions, dreams, and goals of families who are informing school culture and practice. The learning environment is a shared space that cultivates the beliefs, visions, and aspirations of all protagonists involved in learning.

As we reflect on the importance of partnerships in our programs, we should also consider the four types of partnerships outlined by Henderson, Mapp, Johnson, and Davies (2007):

1. Partnership school

2. Open-door school

3. Come-if-we-call school

4. Fortress school

Review the descriptions of these categories in figure 7.2 and ask yourself: Where are you and your school community in this partnership journey? What steps can you take to foster stronger relationships with the families and communities you support?

How and what we communicate lie at the core of our partnerships with families and communities. Effective communication must be reciprocal, respectful, accessible, intentional, and mutually beneficial to children's learning. When parents and educators communicate effectively, we build trust, attain more realistic goals, and deepen our understanding of children, which in turn supports our programming.

Figure 7.2. Four Types of Partnership

Partnership School All families and communities have something great to offer—we do whatever it takes to work closely together to make sure every single student succeeds.	**Open-Door School** Parents can be involved at our school in many ways—we're working hard to get an even bigger turnout for our activities. When we ask the community to help, people often respond.
Come-if-We-Call School Parents are welcome when we ask them, but there's only so much they can offer. The most important thing they can do is help their kids at home. We know where to get help in the community if we need it.	**Fortress School** Parents belong at home, not at school. If students don't do well, it's because their families don't give them enough support. We're already doing all we can. Our school is an oasis in a troubled community. We want to keep it that way.

Source: Text quoted from Henderson et al. (2007, 15).

Family Engagement

Family engagement is a model that centers and promotes families' competencies in a comprehensive fashion. We invite families into a reciprocal exchange of knowledge that values lived experiences that enrich children's development. Families are a gift to be treasured in the early years, as they unwrap learning with us to inspire progressive approaches that move children's thinking.

As we discussed in previous chapters, culturally relevant pedagogy highlights the importance of developing cultural competence, high expectations, and critical consciousness. To enhance our programming, we must build our capacity through the competencies of the families and communities we support. Their funds of knowledge make honorable contributions to our learning spaces. We can hold high expectations of families by viewing them as experts on their children and by valuing their perspectives and contributions. As we learn with and from families, we are led to reflect on and dismantle the biases and assumptions we might hold in our programming. Figures 7.3, 7.4, and 7.5 present a few ways to engage families in the learning space.

Engaging Families in the Learning Space

Figure 7.3. Welcoming all protagonists by offering materials, books, and tools that reflect the lived experiences of multiple identities

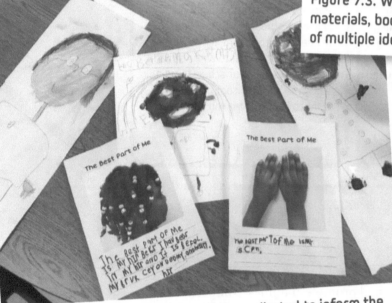

Figure 7.4. A variety of documentation collected to inform the process of learning over time and shared with families for input and insight

The Digital Resources (page 219) include additional examples of how to engage families in various ways in the learning space.

Figure 7.5. Adults exploring loose parts to respond to a question about what they envision for partnership in schooling

Building and Sustaining Connections

We need to recognize that educational spaces might not always be safe places for some learners, families, and communities. We should strive to create braver learning environments through our interactions with children and families. This requires all protagonists to be open to multiple perspectives. We welcome dialogue that allows our intentions to be revealed; however, we must be aware of the potential impact of our words, actions, and deeds. Situate yourself and how you may benefit from unearned societal advantages based on your social identities, such as race, gender, socioeconomic status, ability, religion, ethnicity, language, and sexual orientation. Through courageous conversations and interactions, we can take risks that require us to lean into discomfort to better understand each other.

Traditionally, educators have held the most power within learning spaces, but we can empower learners and families and position them as equal partners in our space by establishing conditions that dismantle these engrained structures. Our interactions may reveal dynamics that shift the sharing of power, and such moments might need to be noticed, named, and challenged with care. We should strive to create a space of trust that respects the integrity of what families share and reveal.

Playful Note

Consider playful approaches to establishing connections with families. You might think about creating vision boards with frames and loose parts to invite families to share their aspirations and dreams, which are then annotated and collectively memorialized within the classroom. Honoring these goals and revisiting them throughout the year creates a space for continuous and meaningful dialogue that centers families.

In our own practice, we have incorporated several strategies for building and sustaining meaningful connections with families and community members, which we share with you here.

Gathering and Incorporating Information about Families

Family questionnaires allow you to collect and gather information about who families and learners are and what they honor. The information gathered from questionnaires provides insights that you can incorporate within your programming. Questionnaires should invite families to share their hopes and expectations, as well as learners' strengths and talents (see a sample on pages 188–189). It is also important to consider that families might not be forthcoming with their answers or willing to disclose information with you for various reasons. We must respect these decisions, but you can also consider offering questionnaires beyond the period of initial contact; as you establish relationships with families, they may be more open to sharing information and insight with you that will support your learning and programming.

Figure 7.6. *All about You* Family Questionnaire

Welcome to our learning community. I am delighted that you will be a part of our community this year as we learn together. My goal is to make our program responsive to the strengths, interests, and needs of the children. I will provide learning opportunities that are aligned with the curriculum and unique cultural experiences to reach the goals of well-being, success, and equity for all children.

I aim to build meaningful partnerships with you, the children, and the community. Your commitment to and participation in this program will be key to the children's success, growth, and development.

Thank you for taking time to provide this important information.

I appreciate your support and partnership!

Please share your child's name:

_____

Child's birthday:

_____

Your name, contact information, and relationship to the child (for example, Nadia Lewis, 123-456-7891, mother):

_____

Special medical information (allergies, asthma, hearing, vision, speech, medications, etc.):

_____

_____

_____

_____

_____

What is your child's country of birth?

_____

What is your child's cultural and family background?

_____

Figure 7.6. *All about You* Family Questionnaire (Continued)

What languages are spoken at home?

_____

What does your child enjoy doing or is interested in?

_____

_____

_____

_____

_____

What are your child's needs (e.g., increased confidence, following instructions, oral language, mathematics, etc.)?

_____

_____

_____

_____

_____

Please share any additional information that I should know about your child in order to ensure their success in the program.

_____

_____

_____

_____

_____

Figure 7.6. *All about You* Family Questionnaire (Continued)

189

As we grow to learn more about families and caregivers, we honor their presence in the learning environment. You can designate an area that shares who lives within the space. This is also a way to remind children of people they love, which can bring them comfort throughout the day. You might invite families to share photos (see figure 7.7 for an example) or invite learners to create artistic representations of people who are important to them. When inviting learners and families to make contributions to the space, it is important to make this an open-ended learning opportunity. Offering specific expectations (e.g., everyone must share a photograph) might silence and exclude certain members of the learning community. Take care to be open, flexible, and responsive.

Figure 7.7. Community Tree

Building Relationships Beyond the Learning Environment

Our communities allow children and families to see that they are connected to a larger network. Experiences that tie families to resources within the community support diverse perspectives in learning. Through the community, protagonists see that connections extend beyond school and home; this leads them to feel a sense of belonging that allows us to partner with them in ways that build and sustain accountable relationships. You can build and sustain these types of connections by incorporating community walks regularly or by leveraging opportunities to learn from others within the community.

The Story of Your Name

Names sometimes reveal the aspirations that families have for their children. As we build connections with families, we should affirm and honor their identities through names because they are sometimes deeply rooted in cultural or spiritual traditions and practices. This requires us to not only learn family members' names but also to pronounce them correctly and ensure that we have not altered or amended them in any way. We might invite families and learners to share the stories of their names by collecting information through questionnaires, through community-engagement events (e.g., "Meet the Teacher," family interviews), or by offering Invitations for Learning where children can share their ideas connected to their names (see the Digital Resources, page 219, for a few examples). You can consider using these children's books for such invitations: *Alma and How She Got Her Name*, *The Name Jar*, *My Name Is Sangoel*, *Your Name Is a Song*, *My Name Is Yoon*, *My Name Is Bilal*, and *How Nivi Got Her Names*.

Family Feedback

We must always look to families to provide us with ongoing feedback that can shift our thinking as we build programming that merges visions for learning. Sharing online feedback forms (see the Digital Resources, page 219, for an example) or engaging in informal conversations with families helps provide perspective on families' hopes, wants, and needs. Family feedback forms are meant to be offered at different points in the year, as these too serve as documentation that can be analyzed over time to see how goals have been met or need to be revisited to reassess strategies for programming. This is not an evaluation but rather provides data to hold us accountable for the work that must be done.

Newsletters create opportunities for dialogue with families and caregivers on a regular basis (for an example, see the Digital Resources, page 219). Prior to creating and sharing a newsletter, consider how you can ensure that it will be responsive to the needs of the learning community and how it will be accessible for everyone (e.g., by being offered in both digital and print formats). Co-creating a newsletter with learners is another way to honor their insight and perspectives about their learning and what they would like to share. As you create your newsletter, consider how it will communicate learning and open and sustain reciprocal dialogue with families and caregivers. Your newsletter should offer opportunities for families to provide input and respond (e.g., by asking questions; by taking polls; by dedicating sections for highlighting parent responses, thoughts, and contributions).

Opening the Doors to Play

Play is as much a vehicle for learning for families as it is for children. Bridging communication through play allows us to harness the potential for learning. When families enter the learning environment, we should strive to offer opportunities for them to engage in play, to affirm and center its importance in our program. Many misconceptions emerge when educators offer play-based programming and families interpret it as "just play." We must become advocates for this pedagogical approach and highlight, notice, and name how play benefits learning and promotes learners' success. Play can also forge pathways to cultural experiences that allow for deeper connections to families and communities. There are many strategies that can open the doors to play for families and the community described on the following pages.

Playful Partnership Programming

Provide opportunities for families to engage in play with their children at Invitations for Learning within the learning environment (see figure 7.8 for an example). This offers access to materials that are new for families but also allows for exchanges where they share what other loose parts they use at home. This is an opportunity for educators, families, and children to notice and name learning and make connections back to the curriculum.

Figure 7.8. Families Engaging in Play in the Learning Environment

Community Engagement Events

There are many opportunities during the year for families, caregivers, and community members to engage in learning together (e.g., Meet the Teacher Night, Open House, Family Literacy Night, STEAM Challenge Night). These events provide platforms for educators to engage families in playful learning opportunities (see figure 7.9). As you plan an event, it is important to ask yourself: How can this event honor and replicate playful experiences that are reflective of play-based approaches?

Figure 7.9. Families Engaging in Learning at a Community Event

Leveraging Loose Parts

Loose parts play an integral role in our programming. Sharing their importance with families invites collection of open-ended materials in the classroom and at home for endless possibilities to play. You can invite learners to gather playful pieces at home that can be used in the classroom, and you can encourage families to create their own collections at home that can be used to extend learning (see figure 7.12 for a sample letter to families). In our own practice, we have honored the importance of playful pieces by offering gifts of loose parts to educators, learners, and families we have partnered with. Figure 7.10 shows an example where a collection of loose parts (gems, wooden peg people, rocks, pictures of structures around the world, wood beads, and sticks) was presented to learners, families, and educators to inspire play and learning at home. The gift included a note describing what the loose parts represented:

> *A pair of wood peg people, to remind you that we are a team, and you will never be alone.*
>
> *Precious gems, because I value our partnership.*
>
> *Rocks, to represent the strong foundation of wonder and learning we will instill in our learners.*

Pictures of places far and wide, to remind you of all the amazing places we'll go together in our learning journey.

Wood beads, to help you roll into this exciting new year.

Sticks to remind you that we will stick together as we engage in dialogue, reflection, and new learning together.

Figure 7.10. A Gift of Loose Parts

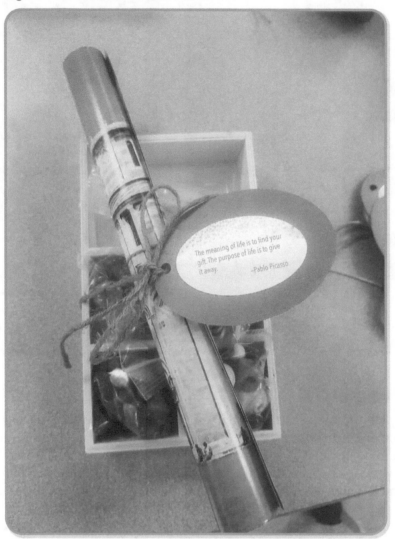

Creating a Family Lounge

A family lounge is a space families can visit to access information, resources, and playful strategies for supporting their children. Figure 7.11 shows a virtual family lounge that has been made accessible to families and caregivers. In the lounge, the poster by Unlearn on the left links to a Jamboard with the question "What does family mean to you?" This offers a place where families can share their ideas on sticky notes by drawing or annotating their thoughts. On the right is a Romero Britto photo that links to another page with the question "What is your wish for your child?" In the lower left, the book *All Are Welcome* by Alexandra Penfold is offered, with a link to a recording of the story. In the lower right, the tablet on the chair presents a link where families can schedule a time to meet virtually with the educator. Within the drawers in the center of the lounge, there are links to information about loose parts, online resources, Invitations for Learning, songs, books shared in class, and more.

Figure 7.11. A Virtual Family Lounge

Offering Invitations for Learning in Community Spaces

We can communicate the importance of play by offering learners, families, and community members the opportunity to engage with Invitations for Learning in various spaces in the school community. You can consider offering Invitations for Learning in areas such as the school office, the school library, or spaces where community events or family meetings might be held.

Partnerships with families can create powerful play experiences throughout the school learning environment that build trusting relationships. We must create welcoming communities that invite all protagonists. We can realize our dreams for a better future for children and the world by shifting our efforts and learning collectively.

Playful Note

Consider Invitations for Learning that can be offered to families to help build powerful partnerships with them. These children's books would work well for such invitations: *All Are Welcome, You Matter, Your Name Is a Song, Dreamers, Lubna and Pebble, The Invisible String, Count on Me, Say Something, Yo Soy Muslim, Counting on Community,* and *Where Are You From?*

Figure 7.12 Sample Letter to Families about Loose Parts

Dear Families,

Thank you so much for supporting our play-based programming. In our classroom, we believe that play is the vehicle for learning, and your child uses materials called *loose parts*.

Loose parts are open-ended materials that can be assembled, combined, or manipulated in a variety of ways to create something new. The possibilities for play and learning with these materials are endless!

As we engage in learning this year, we encourage you and your child to gather materials at home that can be used to support our learning. Here are a few examples:

→ Rocks	→ Toothpicks	→ Cereal boxes
→ Bangles	→ Clothespins	→ Sticks
→ Elastic bands	→ Buttons	→ Beads
→ Gemstones	→ String	→ Yarn
→ Marbles	→ Ribbon	→ Lace
→ Paper clips	→ Fabric	→ Shells
→ Blocks	→ Washers	
→ Hair rollers	→ Keys	

Once your child has gathered these loose parts, have them sort and organize the materials so that they can be brought to our learning community to support their learning. Consider using egg cartons, plastic containers, resealable bags, a shoebox, or bowls to store your materials.

As we participate in learning this year, we will use the loose parts to support our:

→ Literacy learning and comprehension skills

→ Mathematical thinking

→ Creativity and artistic expression

→ Inquiry

→ Problem solving, innovation, and design

We appreciate your support in collecting these materials. We are not expecting families to purchase any items, and we hope that you will simply gather what you already have available at home. If you have any questions or concerns, please do not hesitate to contact me. Thank you for your support as we continue this new learning journey together.

Sincerely,
Your Child's Educator

Additional Considerations

Missed Invitations

Partnership in learning can be a transformative educational experience. In our programs for play-based learning, we center families and learners, who guide and facilitate our planning. As we strive to collaborate, we do have to be mindful that we may need to adjust our ideas and views, as learners or families may challenge our perceptions. As you strengthen partnerships with families, keep these misconceptions in mind:

Missed Invitation 1: "I don't know much about the community, but I know what works best for children's learning."

As educators, we must reflect on our identities and the privileges that we hold. We need to learn who lives within the communities we serve, as they may differ from our own. If we are not responsive to communities' strengths, interests, and needs, we do a disservice to learners. And if we hold assumptions about a particular community, we need to remember that there is danger in making generalizations that negatively affect families and prevent children from achieving academic excellence.

Educators should also be careful to avoid a tourist approach toward the communities they support. Tourists select what they want to explore, when they want to explore it, and how they want to do the exploring. In a tourist mindset, you absolve yourself of being a part of the community; it then becomes easy to assume a savior complex, where you are solely responsible for "fixing" or "saving" families and communities. This negates families' expertise; families should instead be valued as capable and competent.

We must remember that although we may have longstanding relationships with families in the community, this does not mean that our experiences will always be the same. Inherited family legacies often affect our interactions with learners. Regardless of our histories with communities and what we know about children, we must continue to position ourselves as lifelong learners and partners with families and communities. "We have two eyes, two ears, and one mouth so we can watch and listen twice as much as we speak" (Baron and Brooks 2020, para. 1).

Missed Invitation 2: Families continue to question why children are always playing.

Play centers the lived experiences and identities of learners and families. We want to invite families to see the connections and pathways that are created when we offer open-ended materials that allow children to communicate, problem-solve, innovate, collaborate, and think critically. Play-based programming may involve a mindset shift for families and educators whose educational experiences differ greatly from this approach. We must find opportunities to build and sustain relationships that open the doors for families to see the value in play and its developmental and academic benefits. Play is not one-dimensional; it allows for sharing of perspectives and differences in opinion, and it reveals to families a multiplicity of competencies.

Missed Invitation 3: "I'm afraid to address the opposing or challenging views of families, so I just ignore them."

In our learning spaces, we will inevitably face differences of opinion with families and communities. As educators, we have a responsibility to address all matters that arise, whether positive or negative. We must therefore consider how to engage in meaningful and courageous dialogue with families to seek understanding, gain new perspectives, and set shared goals.

Derman-Sparks (2013) shares a three-step protocol for moving through challenging scenarios with families:

1. **Acknowledge:** Recognize that there are opposing thoughts among members of the learning community.

2. **Ask:** Ask questions to gain insight and clarification on the matter.

3. **Adapt:** Seek consensus and create a resolution.

Consider the following questions as you engage in resolution with families:

→ How might this impact the child? What is negotiable?

→ What policies might influence the outcome of this situation?

Unraveling the Knots

Playful partnership with families, children, and community is an educational investment that fosters academic success. As educators, it requires a willingness to listen and learn with intention. We position ourselves as co-learners alongside families; even so, tensions can present themselves in this collaborative process, so we share some knots you may encounter along the way:

Knot 1: The educator is eager to partner with families and the community, but this partnership might trigger memories of trauma associated with schooling.

Trauma can exist within families, which can affect children and the learning community. Sometimes, schooling can be the source of such trauma. As educators, we must continue to develop cultural competency for the communities we partner with. Increased awareness and sensitivity can center the decision for families to empower themselves and seek new avenues for resolution and healing through partnership. Here are strategies to consider:

1. **Empower, never disempower:** Center the voice of families and learners; your educational compass should be guided by their strengths, needs, and wants.

2. **Consistently use a strengths-based approach:** Relationships are based on trust. Take time to learn about families, and communicate with them regularly and in a positive manner. Consider statements such as "You and I both care about your child and want to ensure their success."

3. **Maintain high expectations:** Just as we hold high expectations for learners, we must in turn hold similar expectations for the relationships we can form with families and communities. Treat families in the same way you want your family to be treated.

4. **Be self-reflective:** Trauma can affect communities in a variety of ways. As we aim to partner with families, we must be self-aware of the biases and assumptions we possess. Ask yourself these questions:

→ What biases and assumptions might you hold about families? How is your thinking informed by other sources (e.g., colleagues, the media, previous experiences)?

→ How can you use research to rethink, learn, and act?

5. **Create sustainable partnerships:** Continually strive to build relationships with families. Maintain an open and welcoming stance that provides opportunities for families to partner with you in a variety of ways. Be creative and flexible in your approach.

> When the concept of trauma-informed care is applied in the context of schools, the outcome is an institution that seeks to change the mainstream paradigm from one that asks *what is wrong with you* to one that considers *what happened to you.* When this approach is operationalized, a trauma-informed institution can recognize the presence of trauma symptoms and promote healing environments through trauma-informed practices predicated upon: safety; trust; collaboration; choice and empowerment; as well as building of strengths and skills. (British Columbia Provincial Mental Health and Substance Use Planning Council 2013, as cited in Ontario Federation of Indigenous Friendship Centres 2016, 3, emphasis in original)

Knot 2: We impose our values on learners in opposition to families' beliefs.

Educators care for learners for a large part of the day and may have the best of intentions for them, but at times what we believe is best for children runs counter to families' beliefs. For example, when a learner eats a morning snack provided from home, such as sticky rice, the educator may caution the child and say, "It's too early to be eating such a heavy snack," and determine that it is not to be eaten. In this scenario, the educator has imposed their beliefs about what should be eaten in the morning; the educator has determined that a family's culturally common practice is not acceptable in the learning environment. "While best practices ensure that an approach is useful to some, wise practices ensure that an approach is informed by culture" (Ontario Federation of Indigenous Friendship Centres 2016, 3). The adoption of wise practices within our spaces will influence the success of the learners and move us away from judgmental practices. We must also be mindful that as protagonists (educators, children, and families), what we honor is intentional and does not cause harm to the other children in the learning space.

Pursuing the Gift

Partnerships in play can purposefully drive our practices in teaching. Our learning communities work to enhance our programs for learners. Consider the following shifts to transform your programming:

→ **Seek insight and learn.** Work intentionally to get to know learners and their families. You can do this by establishing daily routines (e.g., greeting families daily, dedicating time at the end of the day for informal conversations). You can also learn about the communities that you partner with; get a sense of where learners and families go to eat, shop, or play. This insight will help you gain a better understanding of families that builds on the information gathered from family questionnaires and feedback forms.

→ **Play, learn, and grow in partnership.** Set aside time for families, learners, and the community to come together and engage in play. This is a great opportunity to make connections to how the play connects to learning, programming, and the curriculum with protagonists.

→ **Plan a playful opportunity that invites family participation.** Consider a book that you intend to read with learners, and think of ways families can be invited to connect to the learning. For example, if you intend to read a book about the importance of names, send a letter home encouraging families to share with children the stories of their names.

Gifts of Learning

In exploring the role of partnerships in the learning journey, we have outlined how families' competencies can be leveraged for learning and programming. To summarize the key concepts explored in this chapter:

→ Families should be seen as partners in education.

→ We can use several key strategies to build partnerships with families.

→ There are four types of partnerships: partnership school, open-door school, come-if-we-call school, and fortress school.

→ We can build and sustain partnerships with families by gathering information from them and incorporating it in our programming, building relationships beyond the learning environment, honoring the stories of their names, and seeking their feedback.

→ We can promote playful opportunities for families and caregivers through playful partnership programming, community engagement events, leveraging loose parts, and offering Invitations for Learning in community spaces.

In this chapter, we have explored how powerful partnerships create strong foundations for play and learning. We invite you to reflect on the following questions:

→ How might you honor and respect the competencies of the families in your learning environment?

→ What strategies can you utilize to foster playful partnerships?

→ How can you engage in meaningful dialogue with colleagues, administrators, and system leaders to make the shifts needed within your school community?

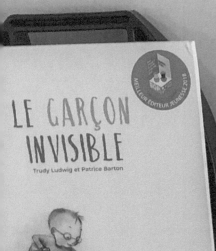

LE GARÇON
INVISIBLE

Trudy Ludwig et Patrice Barton

BE
PROUD !

Learning

Afterword

Dear Educator,

While the journey to pursue and unwrap the gift of learning is not an easy one, we hope that it provokes you to cultivate transformational spaces that elevate thinking. The brilliance and competencies that learners possess are waiting to be uncovered and embraced. We need spaces that respect, nurture, value, and care for learners through play. The antiquated approaches of yesterday will not serve learners of tomorrow. Children deserve spaces where they are seen and heard and where they can access Invitations for Learning that highlight their gifts.

As you embark on this journey, we offer a loose-parts creation on the next page to remind you of the gift play will ignite for you and children around the world.

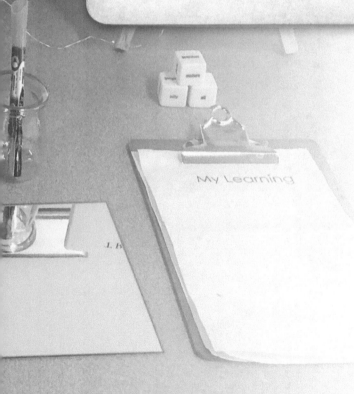

Our loose-parts creation includes:

- Peg people in a circle remind us of the importance of *children, the community, fostering strong relationships*, and *the cyclical nature of learning*.

- Wavy candles represent the *connectivity of ideas*.

- Balloons remind us to *celebrate* the diverse identities, experiences, and skills that play will unleash.

- Feathers highlight the *collective wisdom* that emerges as we share and reflect.

- Gears symbolize the different *tensions and challenges* protagonists might encounter along the learning journey.

We welcome you to take risks, make pedagogical pivots, and shift learning with intention. Prioritizing pathways for play invites you to respond to the needs of children by honoring their identities, interests, and curiosities. Play is a foundation to intentionally merge the curriculum with your insights. Play-based approaches grounded in culturally relevant pedagogy will liberate educational systems that historically have marginalized many communities. Dare to dream and trust in the process.

Trust in play to show you the way!

—Kenisha and Angelique

Children's Literature

Baumgarten, Bret. 2015. *Beautiful Hands*. San Francisco: Blue Dot Press.

Beaty, Andrea. 2019. *Sofia Valdez, Future Prez*. New York: Abrams Books for Young Readers.

Beaumont, Karen. 2004. *I Like Myself!* San Diego: Harcourt.

Bryon, Nathan. 2020. *Rocket Says Clean Up*. New York: Random House.

Bynoe, Kenisha Nadia. 2018. *Shades of Me*. North Carolina: Lulu Press.

Campoy, F. Isabel. 2016. *Maybe Something Beautiful: How Art Transformed a Neighborhood*. New York: Houghton Mifflin Harcourt.

Chocolate, Debbi. 2010. *Kente Colors*. Logan, Iowa: Perfection Learning.

Choi, Yangsook. 2003. *The Name Jar*. New York: Dragonfly Books.

Cornwall, Gaia. 2020. *Jabari Tries*. Somerville, Massachusetts: Candlewick Press.

Cummings, Phil. 2018. *Feathers*. New York: Scholastic Canada.

Engle, Margarita. 2015. *Drum Dream Girl: How One Girl's Courage Changed Music*. New York: Houghton Mifflin Harcourt.

Flett, Julie. 2021. *We All Play*. Vancouver, British Columbia: Greystone Kids.

Genhart, Michael. 2018. *Love Is Love*. Naperville, Illinois: Little Pickle Press.

George, Angela May. 2016. *Out*. New York: Scholastic Canada.

Gomi, Taro. 2017. *I Know Numbers!* San Francisco: Chronicle Books.

Hale, Christy. 2012. *Dreaming Up: A Celebration of Buildings*. New York: Lee and Low Books.

Hall, Michael. 2015. *Red: A Crayon's Story*. New York: Greenwillow.

Harrison, Vashti. 2018. *Festival of Colors*. New York: Beach Lane Books.

Hohn, Nadia L. 2016. *Malaika's Costume*. Toronto: Groundwood Books.

Howes, Katy. 2019. *Be a Maker*. Minneapolis: Lerner.

Hunt, Dallas. *Awâsis and the World Famous Bannock*. 2018. Winnipeg: Portage and Main Press.

Khan, Hena. 2018. *Crescent Moons and Pointed Minarets: A Muslim Book of Shapes*. San Francisco: Chronicle Books.

Ludwig, Trudy. 2013. *Le garçon invisible*. New York: Random House.

——. 2013. *The Invisible Boy*. New York: Random House.

Madison, Megan, and Jessica Ralli. 2021. *Our Skin: A First Conversation About Race*. New York: Penguin Young Readers.

Maier, Brenda. 2018. *The Little Red Fort*. New York: Scholastic.

Meddour, Wendy. 2019. *Lubna and Pebble*. New York: Dial Books.

Méndez, Yamile Saied. 2019. *Where Are You From?* New York: HarperCollins.

Mercurio, Ishta. *Small World*. 2019. New York: Abrams Books for Young Readers.

Murray, Diana. 2016. *City Shapes*. New York: Little, Brown Books for Young Readers.

Nyongo, Lupita. 2019. *Sulwe*. New York: Simon and Schuster.

O'Leary, Sara. *This Is Ruby*. 2021. Toronto: Tundra Books.

Ortner, Nick. 2018. *My Magic Breath: Finding Calm Through Mindful Breathing*. New York: HarperCollins.

Penfold, Alexandra. 2018. *All Are Welcome*. New York: Random House.

——. 2021. *Big Feelings*. New York: Alfred A. Knopf.

Percival, Tom. 2021. *Meesha Makes Friends*. New York: Bloomsbury.

Reynolds, Peter H. 2014. *Going Places*. New York: Atheneum Books for Young Readers.

——. 2018. *The Word Collector*. New York: Orchard Books.

Robinson, Christian. 2019. *Another*. New York: Simon and Schuster.

Robinson, Nikki Slade. 2018. *Anywhere Artists*. New York: Clarion.

Rotner, Shelley, and Sheila M. Kelly. 2010. *Shades of People*. New York: Holiday House.

Ruurs, Margriet. 2016. *Stepping Stones: A Refugee Family's Journey*. Victoria, British Columbia: Orca Book Publishers.

Smith, Kim. 2019. *Boxitects*. New York. HarperCollins.

Spiller, Trudy. 2017. *Trudy's Rock Story*. Victoria, British Columbia: Medicine Wheel Publishing.

Tanco, Miguel. 2019. *Count on Me*. Toronto: Tundra Books.

Thompkins-Bigelow, Jamilah. 2021. *Your Name Is a Song*. Seattle: Innovation Press.

Van Camp, Richard. 2016. *We Sang You Home*. Victoria, British Columbia: Orca Book Publishers.

Williams, Karen Lynn, and Khadra Mohammed. 2009. *My Name Is Sangoel*. Grand Rapids: Eerdmans.

Winter, Jeanette. 2017. *The World Is Not a Rectangle: A Portrait of Architect Zaha Hadid*. New York: Beach Lane Books.

Wood, Audrey. 2001. *Alphabet Adventures*. New York: Blue Sky Press.

Yuksel, M. O. 2021. *In My Mosque*. New York: HarperCollins.

Zwillich, Julie. 2017. *Phoebe Sounds It Out*. Berkeley, California: Owlkids Books.

References

Ackerman, D. 1999. *Deep Play*. New York: Vintage Books.

Baron, J., and T. Brooks. 2020. "Math on the Land." *ETFO Voice* (Fall 2020). etfovoice.ca/feature/math-land.

Bishop, R. S. 1990. "Mirrors, Windows, and Sliding Glass Doors." *Perspectives* 6 (3): ix–xi.

British Columbia Provincial Mental Health and Substance Use Planning Council. 2013. "Trauma-Informed Practice Guide." cewh.ca/wp-content/uploads/2012/05/2013_TIP-Guide.pdf.

Broderick, J. T., and S. B. Hong. 2020. *From Children's Interests to Children's Thinking: Using a Cycle of Inquiry to Plan Curriculum*. Washington, DC: National Association for the Education of Young Children.

Callaghan, K. 2013. *The Environment Is a Teacher*. Toronto, Canada: Ontario Ministry of Education.

Carter, M. 2007. "Making Your Environment 'The Third Teacher.'" *Child Care Information Exchange* (July/August): 22–26.

Cline, B. n.d. "Asking Effective Questions." Chicago Center for Teaching and Learning. Accessed October 29, 2021. teaching.uchicago.edu/resources/teaching-strategies/asking-effective-questions.

Compton, M. K., and R. C. Thompson. 2018. *Story Making: The Maker Movement Approach to Literacy for Early Learners*. St. Paul, MN: Redleaf Press.

Couros, G. 2016. "Beyond Knowing." *George Couros* (blog), September 21, 2016. gcouros.medium.com/beyond-knowing-ffc48032e9f4.

Crenshaw, Kimberle. 1989. "Demarginalizing the Intersection of Race and Sex: A Black Feminist Critique of Antidiscrimination Doctrine, Feminist Theory and Antiracist Policies." *University of Chicago Legal Forum* 1989 (1): 139–167.

Cuffaro, H. K. 1995. *Experimenting with the World: John Dewey and the Early Childhood Classroom*. New York: Teachers College Press.

Curtis, D. 2010. *Creating Invitations for Learning: Supporting Kindergarten*. Saskatchewan Online Curriculum.

Curtis, D., and M. Carter. 2015. *Designs for Living and Learning: Transforming Early Childhood Environments*. St. Paul, MN: Redleaf Press.

Curtis, D., and M. Carter. 2017. *Learning Together with Young Children: A Curriculum Framework for Reflective Teachers*. 2nd ed. St. Paul, MN: Redleaf Press.

Curtis, D., and N. Jaboneta. 2019. *Children's Lively Minds: Schema Theory Made Visible.* St. Paul, MN: Redleaf Press.

Daly, L., and M. Beloglovsky. 2018. *Loose Parts 3: Inspiring Culturally Sustainable Environments.* St. Paul, MN: Redleaf Press.

Derman-Sparks, L. 2013. "Developing Culturally Responsive Caregiving Practices: Acknowledge, Ask, and Adapt." In *Infant/Toddler Caregiving: A Guide to Culturally Sensitive Care,* 2nd ed., edited by E. A. Virmani and P. L. Mangione, 67–94.

Derman-Sparks, L., and J. O. Edwards. 2010. *Anti-Bias Education for Young Children and Ourselves.* Washington, DC: National Association for the Education of Young Children.

Derman-Sparks, L., and J. O. Edwards, with C. M. Goins. 2020. *Anti-Bias Education for Young Children and Ourselves.* 2nd ed. Washington, DC: National Association for the Education of Young Children.

Encourage Play. n.d. "16 Play Types." Accessed January 20, 2022. static1.squarespace.com /static/528e56d6e4b0cf0adc8ecd12/t/5a452a09c830257df7ee98f9/1514482186142/16+play +types.pdf.

Felstiner, S. 2004. "Emergent Environments: Involving Children in Classroom Design." *Child Care Information Exchange* (May/June): 41–43.

Friedman, S., and A. Mwenelupembe. 2020. *Each & Every Child: Teaching Preschool with an Equity Lens.* Washington, DC: National Association for the Education of Young Children.

Gonzalez, J. 2018. "Frickin' Packets." *Cult of Pedagogy* (blog), March 26, 2018. www.cultofpedagogy .com/busysheets.

Gray, P. 2008. "The Value of Play I: The Definition of Play Gives Insights." *Psychology Today,* November 19, 2008. www.psychologytoday.com/ca/blog/freedom-learn/200811/the-value -play-i-the-definition-play-gives-insights.

Hand2Mind. n.d. "Benefits of Manipulatives." Accessed January 20, 2022. www.hand2mind.com /resources/benefits-of-manipulatives.

Hartshorn, R., and S. Boren. 1990. *Experiential Learning of Mathematics: Using Manipulatives.* Charleston, WV: ERIC Clearinghouse on Rural Education and Small Schools.

Haughey, S. 2017. "Loose Parts: Who Is Doing the Thinking . . . The Children or the Toy?" *Fairy Dust Teaching* (blog), March 8, 2017. fairydustteaching.com/2017/03/loose-parts-thinking -children-toy.

Henderson, A. T., K. L. Mapp, V. R. Johnson, and D. Davies. 2007. *Beyond the Bake Sale: The Essential Guide to Family-School Partnerships.* New York: The New Press.

Hughes, B. 2002. *A Playworker's Taxonomy of Play Types.* 2nd ed. London: PlayLink.

Hurston, Zora Neale. 1942. *Dust Tracks on a Road.* Philadelphia: Lippincott.

International Literacy Association. n.d. "Children's Rights to Read." Accessed January 20, 2022. www.literacyworldwide.org/docs/default-source/resource-documents/ila-childrens-rights -to-read.pdf.

Johnson, P. 2006. *One Child at a Time*. Portsmouth, NH: Stenhouse Publishers.

Ladson-Billings, G. 1994. *The Dreamkeepers: Successful Teachers of African American Children*. San Francisco: Jossey-Bass.

Ladson-Billings, G. 1995. "But That's Just Good Teaching! The Case for Culturally Relevant Pedagogy." *Theory into Practice* 34 (3): 159–165.

Malaguzzi, L. 2011. "No Way. The Hundred Is There." In *The Hundred Languages of Children: The Reggio Emilia Experience in Transformation*, 3rd ed., edited by C. L. Edwards, L. Gandini, and G. Forman, 3–4. Santa Barbara, CA: Praeger.

Massachusetts Department of Early Education and Care and WGBH Educational Foundation. n.d. "Build Relationships with Families." Accessed January 20, 2022. resourcesforearlylearning .org/educators/module/20/13/61.

Miller, E., and J. Almon. 2009. *Crisis in the Kindergarten: Why Children Need to Play in School*. College Park, MD: Alliance for Childhood.

Minor, C. 2019. Keynote presentation at ILA Intensive, Las Vegas, NV, June 2019.

Mraz, K., A. Porcelli, and C. Tyler. 2016. *Purposeful Play: A Teacher's Guide to Igniting Deep and Joyful Learning Across the Day*. Portsmouth, NH: Heinemann.

Nell, M. L., W. F. Drew, and D. E. Bush. 2013. *From Play to Practice: Connecting Teachers' Play to Children's Learning*. Washington, DC: National Association for the Education of Young Children.

Nicholson, S. 1972. "The Theory of Loose Parts: An Important Principle for Design Methodology." *Studies in Design Education Craft & Technology* 4 (2): 5–14.

Ontario Federation of Indigenous Friendship Centres. 2016. "Trauma-Informed Schools. 'Ask Me about Trauma and I Will Show You How We Are Trauma-Informed': A Study on the Shift toward Trauma-Informed Practices in Schools." *OFIFC Research Series* 4 (Summer). ofifc.org /wp-content/uploads/2020/03/Trauma-Informed-Schools-Report-2016.pdf.

Ontario Ministry of Education. 2013. "Culturally Responsive Pedagogy: Towards Equity and Inclusivity in Ontario Schools." *Capacity Building Series, K–12*. www.onted.ca /monographs/capacity-building-series.

———. 2015. "Pedagogical Documentation Revisited: Looking at Assessment and Learning in New Ways." *Capacity Building Series, K–12*. www.onted.ca/monographs/capacity-building -series.

———. 2016a. *Growing Success—The Kindergarten Addendum: Assessment, Evaluation, and Reporting in Ontario Schools*. www.edu.gov.on.ca/eng/policyfunding /growingsuccessaddendum.html.

———. 2016b. *The Kindergarten Program, 2016*. files.ontario.ca/books/edu_the_kindergarten _program_english_aoda_web_oct7.pdf.

———. n.d. "Fundamental Principles of Play-Based Learning." Accessed January 20, 2022. www .edugains.ca/resourcesKIN/PLF/TrainingResources/Spring2016Training /FundamentalPrinciplesOfPlayBasedLearning.pdf.

Reimer, Joan, Deb Watters, Jill Colyer, and Jennifer Watt. 2016. *THINQ Kindergarten: Inquiry -Based Learning in the Kindergarten Classroom*. Cambridge, Ontario, Canada: Wave Learning Solutions.

Rinaldi, C. 1998. "Projected Curriculum Construction through Documentation—Progettazione." In *The Hundred Languages of Children: The Reggio Emilia Approach—Advanced Reflections*, 2nd ed., edited by C. Edwards, L. Gandini, and G. Forman. 114. Greenwich, CT: Ablex.

———. 2001. "Documentation and Assessment: What Is the Relationship?" In *Making Learning Visible: Children as Individual and Group Leaders*, edited by C. Giudici, C. Rinaldi, & M. Krechevsky. Reggio Emilia, Italy: Reggio Children.

———. 2013. *Re-imagining Childhood: The Inspiration of Reggio Emilia Education Principles in South Australia*. Adelaide, South Australia: Department of the Premier and Cabinet.

Shalaby, C. 2017. *Troublemakers: Lessons in Freedom from Young Children at School*. New York: The New Press.

Singh, S., and C. Brownell. 2019. *Math Recess: Playful Learning for an Age of Disruption*. San Diego, CA: IMPress.

Stacey, S. 2019. *Inquiry-Based Early Learning Environments: Creating, Supporting, and Collaborating*. St. Paul, MN: Redleaf Press.

Thiel, J. 2014. "Privileged Play: The Risky Business of Language in the Primary Classroom." *Perspectives and Provocations* 1: 1–15.

Thornhill, M. 2015. "Loose Parts and Intelligent Playthings Categorized by Schema." www .countyofrenfrewelcc.com/userfiles/file/10-%20Schema%20theory%20chart1.pdf.

Tomlinson, C. A. 2017. *How to Differentiate Instruction in Academically Diverse Classrooms*. 3rd ed. Alexandria, VA: ASCD.

White, R. 2012. *The Power of Play: A Research Summary on Play and Learning*. St. Paul: Minnesota Children's Museum.

Index

f denotes figure

Digital Resources

Accessing the Digital Resources

The digital resources can be downloaded by following these steps:

1. Go to **www.tcmpub.com/digital**

2. Use the ISBN number to redeem the digital resources.

   > **ISBN: 978-1-0876-4907-8**

3. Respond to the question using the book.

4. Follow the prompts on the Content Cloud website to sign in or create a new account.

5. The content redeemed will now be on your My Content screen. Click on the product to look through the digital resources. All resources are available for download. Select files can be previewed, opened, and shared.
   For questions and assistance please contact Shell Education.
   email: customerservice@tcmpub.com
   phone: 800-858-7339

Contents of the Digital Resources

You will find additional resources that will enhance and support your use of play-based approaches as a vehicle for learning and thinking with young learners.

- → Templates for the forms in this book

- → Sample flow-of-the-day schedules

- → Examples of the components of Invitations for Learning

- → Examples of the use of texts in Invitations for Learning

- → Examples showing how to offer Invitations for Learning